{ FULFILLED }

Living and Leading with Unusual Wisdom, Peace, and Joy

Kirk Byron Jones

Abingdon Press™

Nashville

Library of Congress Cataloging-in-Publication Data has been requested.

ISBN 978-1-4267-5793-8

All scripture quotations unless noted otherwise are taken from the New Revised Standard Version of the Bible, copyright 1989, Division of Christian Education of the National Council of the Churches of Christ in the United States of America. Used by permission. All rights reserved.

Scripture quotations marked "NKJV™" are taken from the New King James Version®. Copyright © 1982 by Thomas Nelson, Inc. Used by permission. All rights reserved.

Scripture quotations marked (ESV) are from The Holy Bible, English Standard Version® (ESV®), copyright © 2001 by Crossway, a publishing ministry of Good News Publishers. Used by permission. All rights reserved.

Scripture quotations marked *GOD'S WORD* are taken from *GOD'S WORD*®. Copyright 1995 God's Word to the Nations. Used by permission of Baker Publishing Group. All rights reserved.

Lucille Clifton, "spring song" from *The Collected Poems of Lucille Clifton*. Copyright © 1972, 1987 by Lucilla Clifton. Reprinted with the permissions of The Permissions Company, Inc. on behalf of BOA Editions Ltd., www.boaeditions.org

"The Avowal" by Denise Levertov, from THE STREAM AND THE SAPPHIRE, copyright © 1984 by Denise Levertov. Reprinted by permission of New Directions Publishing Corp.

Daniel Ladinsky, I HEARD GOD LAUGHING, © 1996 by Daniel Ladinsky. Reprinted by permission of the author.

Pronouns referring to God (such as *he, him, his*) appear lowercased in *Fulfilled*, according to house style.

13 14 15 16 17 18 19 20 21 22—10 9 8 7 6 5 4 3 2 1

MANUFACTURED IN THE UNITED STATES OF AMERICA

Praise for *Fulfilled*

One night, after years as a successful and inspirational minister, Kirk Byron Jones found himself unable to finish a sermon. His quest to discover why he "burned out while trying to be a bright light in the world" led to his discovery of three powerful truths, which changed his life. Read this remarkable book, experience the transformative power of its revelations, and prepare to be fulfilled.

    —Lynn A. Robinson, author of *Divine Intuition: Your Inner Guide to Peace, Prosperity and Purpose* and *Listen: Trusting Your Inner Voice in Times of Crisis.*

Don't read this book unless you are ready to let go of ministry as driven, burdensome, exhausting. Kirk Byron Jones bears witness to a "more excellent way"—a daily practice of living fully into Jesus' promise of abundance. Immerse yourself in these pages, then go and do likewise!

    —Rebecca Youngblood, executive director, The Center for Ministry, Jackson, MS

Facing burnout midway through his ministry, Kirk Byron Jones found life-giving peace, wisdom, and joy through stillness, awareness, and playfulness. *Fulfilled* is candid and hopeful, combining practices easy to use or to modify with a richness and depth informed by music and poetry. Every pastor will identify with his story and can benefit from his guidance and encouragement.

    —Lovett H. Weems Jr., distinguished professor of church leadership and director, Lewis Center for Church Leadership, Wesley Theological Seminary, Washington, DC

Kirk Byron Jones' book *Fullfilled* enters an ongoing conversation about ministerial leaders doing too much. The book then furthers that conversation into a constructive argument for what a fulfilling—rather than a depleting—ministry might be. Jones' seven signs of a pastor who is "running on empty" read like a diagnosis of virtually every leader I know, but reading this book filled my tank! He offers new perspectives, images, and practices that not only will help ministers to thrive but will help them to model sanity in a world of relentless demands.

    —Sarah B. Drummond, dean of the faculty and vice president for academic affairs, Andover Newton Theological School

I love Kirk Byron Jones. His writing resonates with me and reminds me of things my soul craves, but that I too often forget in the midst of my daily life. This book will be a retreat for your soul.

—**Adam Hamilton**, best-selling author and senior pastor, United Methodist Church of the Resurrection

Kirk Jones has written a book for religious leaders—and anyone who is looking to re-discover the magic, melody, and mystery of life. So, relax, fix your favorite cup of "brew," and prepare yourself to be invited into a sacred space where play, imagination, creativity, and holy silence converge in a dance of words, barely able to be contained on the printed page. *Fulfilled* is a work of art drawing the reader into deeper visions of the joy-filled life.

—**Sharon G. Thornton, PhD,** professor of pastoral theology, Andover Newton Theological School

In *Fulfilled,* Kirk Byron Jones offers hope and a sense of possibility to weary pastors. It's both practical and imaginative. His focus on stillness, awareness, and playfulness counters the all-too-common sense that ministry is all about busyness and seriously hard work. I always feel more energy after reading one of Kirk's books, and *Fulfilled* is no exception.

—**Margaret Marcuson,** author of *Leaders Who Last: Sustaining Yourself and Your Ministry*

Kirk is one who has learned how to flourish after facing his own personal challenge with burnout. In *Fulfilled,* Kirk offers wisdom gained from his own journey of faith as he has found ways to restore joy and playfulness to his own call to leadership. Easily accessible and helpful to any leader caught on the hamster wheel who wants off.

—**A. Roy Medley**, general secretary, American Baptist Churches, USA

I'm in awe of the great jazz musicians who've dazzled listeners by jumping with abandon, only to see the net appear out of thin air. Kirk Byron Jones shows pastors (and musicians) how to minimize the stress of "the jump" and add joy to the process, by applying a little SAP beforehand. Read this book and you'll know what I mean.

—**Kirk Whalum**, Grammy award-winning jazz saxophonist

To the Spirit of Relentless Grace
who loves us all so madly

Dear God,

Grant us easy peace
in uneasy vulnerability,

as we fight to resist feeling too comfortable
with too precise understandings of you,

knowing that it is your playful will
to surprise us, over and over again.

Amen.

{ CONTENTS }

{ Acknowledgments }

Another book journey, my tenth, has been completed, and I feel blessed beyond measure. The blessing is a layered one. The first layer is the blessing of writing. I so enjoy the arduous, playful, and mysterious play of thought-catching and word-dancing. More than writing because I know, I write to know. It is a wondrous journey that I genuinely enjoy embarking on, often with jazz playing in the background, more and more.

A second, but by no means less meaningful, layer of blessing is having the excellent and enthusiastic assistance of an outstanding publishing company. Thank you, Abingdon Press staff, for unleashing your vast publishing powers onto *Fulfilled.* I extend a hearty handshake to Len Wilson. As an editor at Abingdon, before moving on to another rich pasture, Len warmly accepted and affirmed my initial ideas for *Fulfilled.*

Among the many at Abingdon Press who have given head and heart to this book is one special champion of an editor. Constance Stella is this writer's dream: a gifted and talented one who feels the heart of what I am trying to say, and assists in such saying, in ways finer and fuller than I would ever alone imagine.

My third layer of blessing is friends and family who have encouraged *Fulfilled*'s entrance into the world through word and deed. I especially thank my students/friends of Andover Newton Theological School's Spring 2013 *Grace Flow* class for engaging the content of this book with relentless interest and joy. I lovingly thank my wife, Mary "Bunnie" Brown-Jones, for continuing to encourage and celebrate my growth as a person, husband, and playful seeker and witness.

Finally, I hope you don't mind me counting you, reader of this book, as a friend in spirit. My prayer is that the words and spaces between the words of my offering, and the words and spaces between the words of your response, blend to form a unique layered blessing for you.

{ Introduction }

There is a space within you that has never known fear.
Go there and receive untold wisdom, peace, and joy to journey on.
—KBJ

In an interview, Gardner C. Taylor, former pastor of Concord Church of Brooklyn, New York, and one of the most esteemed preachers of our time, said to me that there were times in his long tenure when he would rather have been anything else but a minister, even a sanitation worker. Though the startling confession of this ministerial titan jolted me initially, I had been in ministry long enough for his words to settle into a place of understanding acceptance in my spirit. Though soulfully inspiring beyond words, ministry can also leave one limping and looking for something else.

For many, the burden of ministry has something to do with rarely feeling ever fully relieved in ministry. Full contentment is an elusive commodity in a vocation of continual minute and monumental demands and expectations. Ministry can easily leave one with a feeling of missing more than hitting a constantly moving target.

A well-known writer provides a glimpse of the frustration and hope that can be related to ministry. In *The Writing Life,* Annie Dillard tells of a dream she had at a time when she was learning, with limited success, how to split wood:

One night while all this had been going on, I had a dream in which I was given to understand, by the powers that be, how to split wood. You aim, said the dream—of course!—at the chopping block. It is true you aim at the chopping block, not at the wood; then you split the wood, instead of chipping it. You cannot do the job cleanly unless you treat the wood as the transparent means to an end, by aiming past it. ([New York: Harper & Row, 1989], 43)

Pastoral leadership can be a continual tyranny of constantly aiming and missing. At the root of the problem, perhaps, is the nature of pastoral work. Is it ever possible to feel totally accomplished in a job that includes such varied and sundry challenges, many of them at the dangerous and frightful crossroads of personal decision making, change, and loss? And even more daunting than the multitasking nature of the calling is the outrageous presumption. How unrealistic and utterly preposterous is it for one human being ever to think that he or she could ever mediate MYSTERY to another human being?

And if the foregoing clouds weren't enough to make any attempt at pastoral leadership an ominous endeavor, add to it the overloaded and overdriven context in which ministers are called to do what they do. Perhaps there is no better description of our commonly overburdened and much too often frantic existence than the one offered by David Hallowell in his book *Crazy Busy: Overstretched, Overbooked, and About to Snap:*

Being too busy is a persistent and pestering problem, one that is leading tens of millions of Americans to feel as if they were living in a swarm of gnats constantly taking bites out of their lives. All the screaming and swatting in the world does not make them go away. ([New York: Ballantine Books, 2006], 7)

In 1989, Peter B. Vaill used the expression "permanent

white water" to describe the complex, turbulent, constantly changing tides of the time in his book *Learning as a Way of Being*. Nearly twenty-five years later, the permanent white water has turned to permanent white water on white water.

Stress is a punishing, pervasive source of human diminishment. Christian leaders are not immune to the monster of stress and in some ways are more susceptible to its debilitating attacks. Leaders are counted on to provide constant direction and inspiration even as they themselves struggle with recurring bouts of aimlessness and listlessness. The best alternative, as envisioned by some, is to accept the frequent and unsettling roller-coaster nature of leadership—the emotional and spiritual highs and lows—as being an embedded and inevitable fact of the call to lead. Given the nature of the pastoral calling and the seeming nightmare of the cultural context, it would appear the best we can do is chip the wood.

Under the essential weightiness of ministry and unprecedented cultural complexity and stress, many Christian leaders find themselves straining to be inspired and running on empty. Yet, as in Dillard's dream, there is hope. I believe that thriving as leaders hinges on our discovering ways to aim past the wood of specific skills and tasks.

There is a need for a theology and spirituality that can keep up with the constant pressure of our calling and our culture. Intermittent periods of energy boosts at Christian seasons (Christmas and Easter) are not enough to satisfy the need to manage the deep, complex, and unrelenting needs of our time. Is it possible for us to imagine continual sustaining power for ministry? Might we be inspired and enhanced in new ways by a compelling and livable vision of continual lavish spiritual empowerment, the likes and spirit of which are presented in the following verses of scripture?

With joy you will draw water from the wells of salvation. (Isaiah 12:3)

For I will pour water on him who is thirsty, and floods
on the dry ground; I will pour My Spirit on your descen-
dants[.] (Isaiah 44:3, NKJV)

But the water that I shall give him will become in him a
fountain of water springing up into everlasting life. (John
4:14, NKJV)

There is a common thread in these texts that serves as the
inspiration for this book. That theme is not, as you may suspect,
water. Though water is present in all three scriptures, it is the
lavish nature of the water that captures my heart. The biblical
writers don't just see drips, drops, and puddles of water. Isaiah
sees "wells of salvation," "pour[ing] water," and "floods on the
dry ground." For his part, John doesn't quote Jesus as referring to
a cup or bottle of water, but "a fountain of water springing up."
When it comes to empowerment, God is not stingy and does not
lean toward conservation. The goal seems to be a human spirit
saturated and soaked to no end with the Holy Spirit.

I no longer can tolerate the disconnect between the overflowing spiritual sustenance named in these texts and the sense
of barely making it in ministry. The foregoing scriptures present the possibility of living and leading from spiritual and emotional abundance as opposed to scarcity, to live and lead on "Full"
as a way of life, as opposed to "Empty" as a way of life. We were
never meant to be ever straining it and stressing it in ministry.

Fulfilled dares to envision pastoral leadership as always
being mightily sourced by lavishly flowing streams of spiritual
energy. Moreover, because such streams are divinely filled
and refilled by God's love, they are limitless in their power to
continually enliven those who would choose to be so inspired.

Fulfilled is a theology of life and leadership enhancement based on two primary assumptions: (1) Vibrant leadership is not the exclusive procession of the gifted faithful

few, and (2) leadership vitality may be continually sustained and enhanced through the intentional development and integration of three proved sources of creative energy that separately and together cultivate deep and expanding peace, wisdom, and joy. The three energies are Stillness, Awareness, and Playfulness.

Why Stillness, Awareness, and Playfulness? The answer is a personal one.

I have been in ministry for more than forty years, having preached my first sermon at the age of twelve. I have spent more than twenty-five years in pastoral ministry. Midway through, I burned out. After being unable to finish a sermon one night, I began to try to understand how and why it was possible to end up burned out while trying to be a bright light in the world. Two decades later, and looking back on how a healthier spirit and style of ministry were born inside of me, I realized that what had changed me the most were Stillness, Awareness, and Playfulness. They are the three most important transformative influences in my life, as a person and as a leader. Stillness brings peace. Awareness breeds wisdom. Playfulness gives birth to joy.

By Stillness, I mean what that wondrous spirit-person Howard Thurman refers to as a "cessation of inner churning." By Awareness, I mean *deliberate noticing* of the inner life and outer life. By Playfulness, I mean doing for delight's sake. As it stands, I have written a little about each of these realities in prior books. I will say much more about each one of them in this book, discussing, in particular, their extraordinary offerings for those who lead others. And for the first time, I will discuss these three mighty flows of God's grace in relationship to each other, highlighting their uniquenesses and commonalities.

Fulfilled is part testimony, part exploration, and part encouragement. First, I am writing about these three powerful graces because they have truly graced me and continue to do so daily. But equal to that writing inspiration is a compelling curiosity about how stillness, awareness, and playfulness dance with each other. By writing this book, I am heeding the admonition to write a book that I have sought and not found, and one that I would dearly want to read. As far as I know, though much has been written about each of our magnificent subjects, this is the first book that seeks to understand them in relationship to each other. The undergirding goal for the book is to encourage all who read to consider appropriating these resources in ways that cultivate peace and power.

Indeed, the convergence of stillness, awareness, and playfulness may yield magnificence. On a Tuesday evening in late August 2001, Pulitzer Prize–winning trumpeter and composer Wynton Marsalis was playing at the Village Vanguard, one of the world's most famous jazz clubs. David Hajdu was there to see, hear, and relay an extraordinary moment after someone's cell phone went off as Marsalis played a ballad, "I Don't Stand a Ghost of a Chance with You."

> Marsalis paused. . . . The cell-phone offender scooted into the hall as the chatter in the room grew louder. Still frozen at the microphone, Marsalis replayed the silly cell-phone melody note for note. Then he repeated it, and began improvising variations on the tune. The audience slowly came back to him. In a few minutes he resolved the improvisation—which had changed keys once or twice and throttled down to a ballad tempo—and ended up exactly where he had left off: "with . . . you . . ." The ovation was tremendous. (David Hajdu, "Wynton's Blues," *Atlantic Monthly,* March 2003, 44)

CHAPTER ONE

{ DISTILLING STILLNESS }

The exquisite risk to still our own house. . . .
—St. John of the Cross

Sometimes you need to sit and think. Sometimes you need to just sit.
—Satchel Paige

[A place] of not-thinking, not-remembering, not-wanting.
—Mary Oliver

Why Stillness Makes Me Weep

I am used to it now: crying during my morning times of stillness. It doesn't happen all the time; when it does I just let the tears come. Why do I cry?

Sometimes, I cry at the point of having touched a moment of burdenlessness. There are spaces and places in stillness where I feel as light as a feather. All burdens, worries, and cares are lifted, at least temporarily, and it's as if I can just float away if I choose to do so. It is a moment of being fully relieved of all I've been carrying. I cry for the relief I am feeling and, I think, in

1

part for the realization that I had been carrying all I had been carrying. Sometimes we don't know how much we are bearing until we drop the heavy load. Considering the weight for the first time is enough to make me cry sometimes.

Sometimes I cry from a sense of having bumped into myself, my truest, deepest self, free and unmasked. The roles we fill in life can camouflage, and sometimes compromise, who we are at our essence. It is possible to be so busy trying to be so many things to so many people that we lose a sense of who we are without reference to others and their expectations. In stillness, as all others and all expectations are gathered together for a time in a merciful waiting area outside my consciousness, someone whom I may not recognize at first glance appears. The someone turns out to be me: the me who is me unadorned by all. When I feel a sense of my deepest self, free from all expectations, dependencies, and false identities, I cry. This me feels whole from the inside out. He does not exist for acceptance; he exists from acceptance. He has no need whatsoever to overdo and overreach in order to fit in, because he has been outfitted from within, in a beautiful and comfortable robe of unconditional love.

Coming into mysterious contact with the source of such love is another reason for my crying. I have come to believe in a God of lavish love, grace, and mercy. I know that this love is real because in some moments of stillness majesty, I feel love all over me. When the love is all over me, I am . . . I am in heaven . . . and I cry. Feeling God's love—and listening to Ella Fitzgerald sing and Louis Armstrong play—is the best proof I have for the existence of God. Blessing on blessing, there are moments when I sense where the love is coming from: a Presence whose grace is as relentless as the world can sometimes be heartless. This Presence comforts and empowers me afresh with one of my best truths of all: amid all the worrying and wounding, there is set free in the world a Spirit of Relentless Healing that will not be stopped, no matter what.

So, in those moments of feeling fully released of all burdens, or feeling that I have come into the company of myself, or feeling filled to overflowing with God's love, I cry. And there is a rainbow amid the tears. Thus, many more days than not, I take what St. John of the Cross referred to as "the exquisite risk": the risk of surrendering our deepest heartfelt space to the sway of a Spirit, most holy, chancing that the sightings will be worth the surrender. Mark Nepo offers more helpful light on the best risk of all in *The Exquisite Risk*:

> The exquisite risk is a doorway, then, that lets us experience the extraordinary in the ordinary. It is always near. Truth opens it. Love opens it. Humility opens it. And if stubborn, pain will intensify to open it. Sadness can open it, if felt to its center. Silence and time open it, if we enter them and don't just watch them. ([New York: Three Rivers Press, 2005], 15)

The Secret Sensational Power of Stillness

Be still, and know that I am God.—Psalm 46:10 (ESV)

Silencing our mental chatter is arguably the most important practice of all when it comes to creating, managing, and sustaining a fulfilling life. Here's why. When we are thinking about this and that, we are living a small, albeit splendid, dimension of ourselves. No matter how meaningful and vital our rational thinking is, it's never all we are.

Think of your mental self as being the tip of a majestic iceberg. Stay with the iceberg image. Though its tip is what is seen, its larger mass lies unseen, submerged under water. Moreover, the vast ocean surrounding its mass is yet another portion of its expansive reality. Similarly, your conscious mind is the tip of your total being. Your greater submerged mass is commonly referred to as the subconscious mind, the place where hidden knowledge is stored. But there is even more to us. The water surrounding our conscious and subconscious minds is God's Mind: limitless creative wisdom flowing playful and free, far beyond what the eyes can ever see or the rational mind alone can ever perceive. Maybe this is why Jesus says in John 4:14, "The water I will give will become in you a fountain of water springing up into everlasting life."

Photo courtesy: Istock.

When we limit ourselves to just our thinking, our mental chatter, we are missing out on the dynamism and wisdom of our deeper and wider sacred dimensions. How do we explore these amazing, yet unsung and unseen, dimensions? We explore them through stillness and silence. Quiet the mind through silent prayer, meditation, or just being still and empty in the moment, and all God's enchanting universe opens wide and wonderful for holy adventure.

What David said about being still is truer than most of us ever allow ourselves to know. But, should we choose to,

4

we can know and marvel and revel daily in such unspeakable knowing.

Stillness is no joke, or just maybe the biggest reason of all to laugh and leap for joy!

Stillness as Communion with Mystery

Some of the most provocative words I've read on mystery are not found in a book of theology, but rather an article entitled "We Are Explorers: In Search of Mystery in Videogames" by Tevis Thompson. Consider the following quotations from the article:

> My favorite videogames . . . stay with me after I stop playing. They resonate with mystery. . . .
>
> Mystery, like art, cannot be exhausted. It deepens with reconsideration. A well I draw from again and again. Replay is required. . . . Mystery demands second quests. . . .
>
> Mystery resists closure. It resists completion and clean getaways. It, instead insists. I'm not done with you yet. . . .
>
> Mystery, not mastery, breeds love. I do not love a game because I have conquered it. . . .
>
> Mystery is not merely the unknown. It is the impossibility of knowing and yet the continual attempt to know. (Guest Editorial, Kotaku.com, Oct. 26, 2012)

Such words may cause you to think about video games more deeply than you thought valuable or possible. I thought them well placed here to create some play-like excitement in you for the wonder that is mystery. Thankfully, mystery is available to gamers and non-gamers through stillness. When we pause the movement of mind, we are able to relax more easily in the bosom of the unknown. Such a place is an astounding space of blessing and grace, and no small risk. For what we are kissing when we are kissing mystery in stillness is something that is on Its own terms and not ours. Yet, in the embrace of the accepting unknown, it is possible to be more enthralled than troubled, and more excited than terrified. *As we commune with Mystery in moments of silence and stillness, suddenly new worlds appear, and more, far beyond our safe and familiar dreams, becomes possible and desirable.*

Being Present to Presence

Ever since childhood, I have had an abiding sense of A PRESENCE, A REALITY, other than the world into which I was born. I remember waking up at night when I was a child and just lying in bed feeling and wondering about SOMETHING OTHER. Sometimes, the feeling was so intense I became frightened. On some nights, I remember becoming so disturbed that I yelled out to my parents. I recall a few times trying to cry out to them and not being able to. It was as if for that moment, I had mysteriously been rendered speechless.

My fear about the PRESENCE was calmed by parents who spoke easily of God, A HOLY LOVING MYSTERY. My experience, joined with parental and church influences, inspired a calling to ministry when I was twelve. I was a boy preacher. At twenty-two, I became pastor of my first church, and soon after I started teaching at a local seminary. The common thread uniting my ministry experiences was an abiding sense of the PRESENCE and a feeling of being warmly blessed in my pursuits. Often while preaching, pastoring, and teaching, I felt especially inspired, empowered, and grateful. These were, and are, the times when the PRESENCE winks. These are the times when delightful absorption with what we are doing when we are doing it makes our souls sing and God smile.

While mysterious presence can be experienced anyplace, anytime, and anywhere, I have come to own as most precious those moments of experiencing God in stillness when all thoughts are silenced. Such times allow me to experience God on God's own terms and not my own. Moreover, stillness of mind and heart signifies a willingness on my part to receive God in imaginings and understandings that may have nothing whatsoever to do with my previous understandings of God. My stillness is the offering of a clean slate to God. It is the yearning for God, if God wills, to sing unto me a new song.

This daily desire to engage and be engaged by God (God beyond perception) beyond "god" (the god of my perception) ensures that spirituality is always more than our manufactured constructs. Such an audacious presumption—to know God—is the impossible possibility that is at the highest heights and deepest depths of spiritual aspiration. There is an Unseen Bearer of Pastoral Burden-Bearers who speaks in an unusually calming whisper, saying, "I am with you, and together we will make it through."

Regular intervals of sweet sustained stillness can enhance our awareness of person and potential as a Children of God. Knowing better who we are fuels and fills us to play and soar in ways beyond our wildest imaginings. So endowed, ours is a present and future of not only surviving through it all, but also thriving through it all.

Befriending Stillness

In order to observe more inner calm and peace, we must come to terms with our conscious and unconscious negative valuations of stillness. For example, we associate stillness with mischief. If younger children are too quiet in a home, an alarm may go off inside of us: "What in the world are they up to?" At other times, stillness is used as a punishment: "Sit down and don't you move a muscle!" Sometimes we punish persons who have offended us by giving them "the silent treatment." Another example of a negative perception of stillness is our discomfort with extended pauses in conversation. Finally, we may associate quiet with trying personal life situations. I remember a seminary student linking her uneasiness with stillness with "the calm just before the storm" of another abusive assault from her father.

Though sometimes painful, identifying ways in which stillness has been negatively experienced is a way of preparing stillness to wear new garments, to take on greater positive meaning and value in our still-thirsty lives.

We receive what we deeply desire; what we focus on is what expands in our lives. Consequently, you will not realize more stillness and the resulting peace of mind and soul in your life unless you truly want it. Warning: given that our society promotes noise and busyness, you will have to develop a deep desire for stillness in a hostile environment. It is possible to do this by periodically reminding yourself of the amazing life-transforming benefits of stillness. I encounter people from all walks of life, from all parts of the world. Many are eager to tell of their own transformational experiences with stillness. Here are just a few:

1. Calm
2. Soul Refreshing
3. Hearing God's Voice
4. Acceptance
5. Release
6. Insight
7. Clarity

8. Soulfulness
9. Surprises
10. Originality
11. Connection to God, Self, Nature, and Others
12. Contentment
13. Elation
14. Lavish Grace
15. Inner Spaciousness
16. Courage to Face Fear
17. Creative Energy
18. Noticing More
19. Patience
20. Stretching

Take a moment to reflect on each stillness blessing and its meaning for you, past, present, and future. How have you experienced stillness? Can you think of a moment when being still was especially helpful and meaningful? How do you think you would benefit from having more stillness moments in your day?

Be Still for Clarity, Change, and Contentment

When we are constantly busy, no matter how important the tasks, we risk never really knowing who we are, what we want, and where we are going. Take time to be still in order to know, to become genuinely familiar with your vast inner wealth.

Busyness leads to weariness, and weariness leads to stagnating repetition. In our tiredness, we begin to repeat the same thoughts and behaviors because we don't have the energy for creativity and innovation. Rest leads to peace; peace leads to clarity; clarity leads to creativity. We do not need to rest merely for refreshing and restoration. We need to rest for energy to begin new explorations, to hold in balance the tensions we encounter as leaders, and to take bolder risks on the enchanting journey of sacred transformation. Without rest, we are devoid of the potent energy required for real change.

The best rest includes a feeling of contentment: a sense of peaceful satisfaction about what we have already accomplished, including the lessons we've learned from our mistakes and so-called failures. Some persons resist allowing themselves to feel content for fear of becoming complacent. Remember this distinction: contentment receives new dreams and visions; complacency rejects new dreams and visions.

THE CIRCLE OF REST

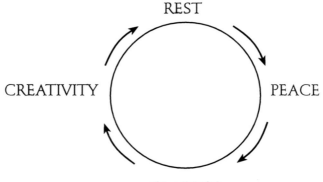

REST

CREATIVITY

PEACE

CLARITY

Rest Leads to Peace.
Peace Leads to Clarity.
Clarity Leads to Creativity.

In order to press on with enhanced clarity and strength, we must pull back with deliberate intention and confidence. And, when you do, allow yourself to feel blessed in the deep places. Let yourself down easy in the soothing waters of God's grace. There are few things in life more dynamic than a rested body and a rested soul. This rest is the sweetest rest of all, the longing for which is beautifully expressed by David in Psalm 42:1: *"As a deer longs for flowing streams, so my soul longs for you, O God"* (GOD'S WORD).

Letting the Fire Lean into You

Before I write, I light a candle. The flame keeps me company and inspires me. I say the flame. In fact, sometimes it's two flames: one candle with two wicks. Though a candle may have two wicks, I usually light only one. The second flame derives from my turning the lit wick toward the direction of the unlit one. Leaning the lit flame toward the other is what causes the unlit wick to catch fire. All the unlit flame has to do is be still.

The Bible uses fire in reference to ecstatic and very personal experience with God. Perhaps the most famous flames are in the burning bush on the back side of the desert that catches the attention and soul of Moses, the invigorating, pulsating, spiritual energy that burns in the prophet Jeremiah so it feels "just like fire" in his bones, and the tongues of sparks that take up residence just above the newly raised heads of renewed Jesus people on the Day of Pentecost. Spirituality in such moments is no staid, static sort of thing; it is the energy of God so vibrant and full that it cannot contain itself within itself. It catches fire, catching everything in its path by fulfilling and thrilling scorching surprise.

What if there is a fire that does not consume, that never goes out? What if there is flame that is always leaning toward us and longing for us to catch fire?

11

{ STILLNESS WAYS }

Silence is God's first language.
—St. John of the Cross

A Direct Path to Peace

Stillness is the most direct path to the peace that is always around and within us. I believe this is true for two reasons: the listening and releasing power of stillness.

Stillness calls us to listen. Stillness allows us to better hear and feel the peace that is the sacred undertone of everything that was, is, and ever will be. Thus, stillness enables us to more readily pick up peace: the everlasting signal of serenity that is always emanating from God. I believe this divine undisturbed peace has never been nor ever can be diminished. Just as important for us is the fact that this peace envelops us. We can only know this to be true by listening and leaning into its truth.

By the way, by using the very same letters, "listen" spells "silent."

I believe stillness is the most direct path to peace because it calls us to release. When you practice breathing, half of your action involves exhaling or letting go. That was and is always a risk on our part. But it is the risk that enriches. Only through releasing breath do we make room for fresh breaths of air. Releasing is refreshing. Similarly, by facilitating a relinquishing of life's stresses, silence opens us up to fresh peace, God's continuing pure peace undiluted by the troubles of this or any other world.

If peace is in God, then it is ever present. Our challenge, therefore, is not to make peace as in create peace, but to more consciously, intentionally, and regularly practice peace. Our challenge is to make peace with peace, to make peace with the peace that already is and always will be. Inner spaciousness and peace breed outer spaciousness and peace.

Limitless Imagination Lavishly Open to Loving Grace

One day, I had a mighty mental impression during a time of soul quiet. There was a house that was closed shut. Suddenly, an angelic presence, more feminine than masculine, appeared and began moving about, freely flinging doors and windows wide open. Light and air filled what was dark and void. This impression moved me with its suddenness and vividness and has remained effortlessly free and full in my memory ever since.

Immediately, I began reflecting on what I saw and felt in that moment. The interpretation was as sure as the impression. I knew that I was the house. I was the one being opened up. Perhaps I knew this because I felt unusually broadened and widened. The impression has had continuing impact. In fact, whenever I am feeling shut in and shut down, in my solitude, I summon My Angel of Open Doors and Windows.

Being and remaining open are a choice, one that we have to make continually. One way to do this is to resist constructing idol gods. Such idols come in all shapes and sizes. An idol god may be a default idea that we have long since stopped questioning. The most dangerous ideas and ideals of all are the ones we never think to question. Sometimes disappointment and despair are reigning idols of the moment. They are raised as we forget that new opportunities and possibilities are forever forming. Maybe the most powerful idol god of all is our notion of God. God is always beyond our best understanding of divinity: god. Holding on to the distinction between God and god keeps us open to the God who moves in mysterious and marvelous, if at times initially unacceptable, ways. On the contrary, god's motions are deathly familiar and, though usually comfortable, are rarely newly enlivening.

Another sure way to be open is to host stillness, which has a way of cultivating spaciousness of heart. Such spaciousness allows for room to grow and can do something else of no small value, writes Gretel Ehrlich in *The Solace of Open Spaces:* "Space has a spiritual equivalent and can heal what is divided and burdensome in us" ([New York, Penguin Group, 1985], 14).

Thinking Empty

Let me face at the outset what I believe is the greatest stumbling block to practicing stillness: believing that it is overly difficult. Our beliefs can either free us or fool us. Don't be duped; most persons have a greater capacity for mental stillness than they know, especially as we become aware of the many stillness-making helps. One great help is your imagination. For instance, close this book, or turn your e-reader over, and for a few moments see an empty page before you.

For as long as you were able to focus on that empty page, you were stilling your mental chatter. The trick or gift wasn't just your ability to focus but what you were focusing on. Whatever we focus on magnifies in our minds. The fact that you were

15

focusing on emptiness allowed you to enter a space Mary Oliver refers to as "not-remembering, not-thinking, and not-wanting."

Focusing on emptiness has become an effective means of entering stillness for me. One of the treats of this method is that I have all sorts of emptiness images to choose from, not all of them having to be figments of my imagination. At my desk, focusing on an empty vase, bowl, or cup has helped me to feel more spaciousness in my soul. Outside, a clear sky and the spaces between tree branches have mediated stillness of mind and heart to me.

Stillness is more reachable than we think, especially as we develop the capacity to imagine and think "empty." In the book's introduction, I challenged getting used to leading and ministering on "E" for empty: being devoid of sufficient fuel needed to satisfy the demands of ministry. But there is another empty that stands in stark contrast to spiritual, emotional, and mental dearth. Indeed, it is just the opposite. This is the emptying of soul space-making, that we may be filled full to running over each day with new mercies and fresh grace.

Morning B.R.E.W.: A Daily Stillness Ritual

One of the most powerful discoveries of my life has been what I lovingly refer to as my morning BREW. I have written an entire book about it, to which I refer you for a more intensive discussion of its benefits and powers. B.R.E.W. is an acronym for Be still; Receive God's love; Embrace yourself, others, and all of creation; and Welcome the day or moment.

1. *Be still.* With the assistance of candlelight and soft music, spend some of your early morning in a state of soul-quiet. One way to simply and effectively do this is to imagine something empty, for example, an empty vase, picture frame, or house. This moment of early-morning emptiness allows you to begin

your day stress free and opens your mind to receive fresh ideas and perspectives.

2. *Receive God's love.* We spend so much of our energy trying to earn acceptance through meeting expectations and pleasing others. The process can be an endless tyranny because no matter how hard we try, we can't do everything and we can't please everyone, making complete acceptance seem impossible. What's the solution? Stop trying to earn your acceptance based on what you do; simply receive it based on who you are: God's child! Stop living for acceptance. Start living from acceptance. One way to feel deep inner acceptance is to imagine yourself floating in soulfully soothing waters of unconditional love.

3. *Embrace yourself, others, and all of creation.* The late, great singer Ray Charles had a habit of throwing both arms around himself and rocking from side to side when he was truly happy. Take some moments each morning to embrace life. Imagine yourself hugging loved ones, new challenges, and yourself. If you can't hug you, how can you expect anyone else to?

4. *Welcome the day or moment.* Acknowledge each new day with a gesture of acceptance and appreciation. Affirmations are an effective welcoming strategy. Here are three of my favorite affirmations: "Today, I will play and soar in the spirit." "I will live this day at a sacred savoring pace." "This is the day I make God laugh out loud."

I spend five to ten minutes performing each step, relying heavily on visualization. For example, during my time of being still, I often envision an empty vase or sky to help me be free of all mental thoughts. This is a time of great ease-making, and for these moments of intellectual freedom and abandonment, God is God on God's terms and not mine. Receiving God's love involves my experiencing God's lavish affirmation by us-ing my imagination to swim in an ocean or sit under a waterfall of God's love. Embracing myself, others, and creation has me offering mental blessings to these wondrous realities and expressions of God. It allows me to enter into the day with an attitude of compassion and kindness toward life, beginning with myself. Finally, the act of intentionally welcoming the day is my way of remembering that life itself is a blessing and nothing that I saw coming or am entitled to based on anything that I've done. This is a way of stirring up gratitude inside me. And, where there is much gratitude, there is less room for complaint and discontent.

Peace Pockets:
Making Peace During the Day

Peace pockets are five- to fifteen-minute intentional intervals throughout the day for spiritual, mental, and physical respite and renewal. During your peace-pocket time, you may listen to soft music, watch a burning candle, pay attention to your breathing, allow your mind to wander free, or give it the freedom not to wander anywhere or think of anything at all. The goal is to be "off" for a moment. The more experience you build, the better you will become at observing your peace pockets. Here are four things to remember as you create your unique and soulfully refreshing peace pockets.

1. *Permission.* If you don't value your calm, no one else will. You have to become convinced of the meaning and value for peace in your own life. You have to become persuaded that you are a better person with peace than without peace. Convince yourself that stillness leads to peace, peace leads to clarity, and clarity leads to creativity. Should you begin to feel guilty and selfish about making more time for nothing, dare to believe that the deeper selfishness is not giving yourself such time. As long as you remain "crazy busy," you ensure that the world, including those nearest and dearest to you, will never behold you at your finest. That would be selfish.

18

2. *Planning.* Schedule daily and weekly times of stillness, and be open to the unscheduled graces of free time simply to be. Planning them with the same intent that you plan your work signals to your consciousness and, just as important, your unconscious mind that claiming your inner calm is as important to you as anything else in your life. As you place these pockets in your calendar, be sure you give them the same level of priority that you give to your most important meetings.

3. *Practice.* Don't just plan your minirespite; live it. Real change involves more than knowing you need to change, wanting to, and planning to. As valuable as that is, authentic change transcends awareness and desire. Real change is actually choosing to be different, to live differently. And sustaining true change involves trusting your transformation beyond all fear and suffering. It will help for you to partner with a friend to serve as a peace support person for the other. Agree with each other to share how you have been intentionally exploring and practicing inner peace. You may want to schedule a "biweekly peace summit" at a restaurant or park to compare notes and celebrate peaceful hearts.

4. *Personhood.* Know that having regular periods of stillness helps you to remember that you are infinitely more than what you do. You are God's "fabulous you" apart from any accomplishment or achievement. God cannot love you any more than God loves you right now, not because of anything you have done or will do. Sometimes coming home to you means savoring moments of having nothing to do.

Stealing Away: The Unsung Preeminent Task of Leadership

One of the most beautiful songs you'll ever hear, no matter what your musical tastes, is "Steal Away" sung by Kathleen

Battle on her enchanting CD, *So Many Stars*. Her voice, Cyrus Chestnut's and the late Grover Washington Jr.'s playing, and the moving lyrics make for an exquisite play-it-again presentation.

Whenever I listen to that song (I am listening now as I write), I think of how intentional we must be if we are to experience moments of soul-easing in times that try our souls. If we are not careful and mindful, we can go through an entire day doing important things and not take a moment to breathe, to ease up, to be still, to rest that we might be renewed and restored. We need sufficient unrushed time and uncramped space in our lives for new ideas to simmer, surface, and be seen.

As committed and satisfied as we may feel, the reality is that we have not only shortchanged ourselves, but we have shortchanged others. At best, due to our depleted state, persons are always receiving a part of us. A depleted self, no matter how devoted, is still a depleted self. This is why self-care is such a benevolent act. It ensures that the world and the people in it, more often than not, receive our best selves and not our soul-diminished and famished imposters.

Taking a moment each day before the day is done to ease our souls down in the soothing waters of God's healing love can make a world of sacred creative difference. Moreover, I have found that such a soaking of soul, first thing in the morning, can set the mood for liberating and empowering love for the entire day.

Living from love, filled with love, is the essential prerequisite for leadership, particularly pastoral leadership, that we rarely talk about. How is it possible to offer love if we don't have love, if we ourselves don't feel loved, aren't filled with love continually? The presumption, you may suspect, is an understanding of service that suggests one must be served first in order to serve well. I am convinced now that the first task of ministry is not to give anyone anything. The first calling of ministry is to receive and revel in God's precious love, each day, several times a day, especially at the start of the day. Stealing away to be renewed by God's love is the necessary prerequisite to offering God's love to others.

The first calling of ministry is not to give away; the first calling, the preeminent task of ministry, is stealing away. Stealing away is what fuels and flavors everything else we do in the Name and Spirit of Love. The prize for stealing away is a heart stolen away, in the most honorable sense of the word, by God.

Poetry: A Sure Bridge to Stillness

[Special note: If you are not a fan of poetry, you may be tempted to skip the next several pages. I beg you to resist the temptation. If you are reading this book, you are most likely a leader. Because you are a leader, your way with words is invaluable. Poets are word mages. Even if you don't usually go in for poems, take the next few moments to read and consider how and why it is that reading just a little poetry, on an irregular basis even, can make a substantive positive difference in how you come across to people in private conversations, meetings, and public presentations.]

In *When God Is Silent*, Barbara Brown Taylor says that Christianity is an "overly talkative religion" ([Boston: Cowley Publications, 1998], 74). She offers the following by way of remedy:

> In a time of famine typified by too many words with too much noise in them, we could use fewer words with more silence in them. This is a difficult concept to grasp, but you know it when you hear it. Some of the most effective language in the world leads you up to the brink of silence and leaves you there, with the soft surf of the unsayable lapping at your feet.

21

I smile on the outside and on the inside when I read Taylor's words. The final phrase of her quotation is her living giveaway as to the kind of language more than any other kind of language that may lead one to the brink of silence: "with the soft surf of the unsayable lapping at your feet." Such language is the language of poetry.

One of the greatest influences of all on my deepening appreciation for stillness, and the silence that may be had more readily there, is poetry. The fact that poetry's power in this regard is explainable doesn't render it any less amazing. First, I find that I have to slow down to read poetry effectively. To rush the reading of poetry is to risk missing its lavish wealth, which leads to the second power of poetry: its optimal use of the meanings and sounds of words. Because poets use fewer of them, they don't waste words. On the contrary, they work wonders with them, evoking the deepest of meaning with just a few carefully selected and placed words—joined by pauses. And this for me is the third power of poetry: pauses. In prose, word follows word, with punctuation marks sometimes effectively causing us to stop. In prose, we pause to breathe just long enough to move on. The moving on is so popular, it has its own term and clientele: speed-reading.

Unless the poetry is especially meant to be said or read at an accelerated pace, such as the kind you hear at some hip-hop slam events, poetry is read more slowly than prose, and pauses are not just rendered via punctuation but through actual space. In poetry, like music, and unlike much prose, pauses are not breaks in the presentation; pauses are integral elements of the presentation, as significant as the words themselves.

I smile an affirming smile before Taylor's words because I have felt "the soft surf of the unsayable" lapping at my feet and suddenly found myself in a corridor of contemplation leading to the altar of stillness. Some of my experiences have become hall of fame moments for me. One such moment was while traveling by plane. The following stanza from Mary Oliver's "Work" stopped me in marvel in my tracks:

> *Sparrows swing on them, they bend down.*
> *When the sparrow sings, its whole body trembles*
> ([New York: DaCapo Press, 2000], 10)

The trembling sparrow touched a deep need in me to know the place of trembling in my own life-song. It also inspired a commencement address delivered at Andover Newton Theological School in Spring 2001 entitled "Ministers Who Sing and Tremble." You may read it online at www.kirkbjones .com or in my book *The Jazz of Preaching: How to Preach with Great Freedom and Joy* (Nashville: Abingdon Press, 2004).

Denise Levertov's "The Avowal" once and a few times more placed me in the holy places that it presents:

> *As swimmers dare*
> *to lie face to the sky*
> *and water bears them,*
> *as hawks rest upon air,*
> *and air sustains them,*
> *so would I learn to attain*
> *freefall, and float*
> *into Creator Spirit's deep embrace,*
> *knowing no effort earns*
> *that all-surrounding grace.*
> (New York: New Directions, 1997)

I love the poetry of the legendary giants of Persia, Hafiz and Rumi. Their love songs to life, love, and mystery as translated by Daniel Ladinsky and Coleman Barks are marvelous for setting the soul at ease and allowing the heart to relax in longings for that which feeds it and makes it whole. Not only are their words profound, but often they are so in lighthearted and imaginative sorts of ways. In "My Brilliant Image," Hafiz hears the sun compliment humanity on

> *The Astonishing Light*
> *Of your own Being!"*
> (*I Heard God Laughing: Poems of Hope and Joy,*
> trans. Daniel Ladinsky [New York: Penguin Books,
> 1996], 7)

In "Quietness," Rumi speaks of silence as a kind of death that brings new life and love. Once we have dared to escape the "frantic running from silence," we can behold the wonder of the "speechless full moon" (*Rumi: The Book of Love,* trans. Coleman Barks [San Francisco: HarperSanFrancisco, 2005], 33).

Finally but no less fabulously, there is the poetry of the late, majestic Lucille Clifton. *The Collected Poems of Lucille Clifton* is one of my most prized possessions. Making my way home from the bookstore after purchasing the beautiful volume, I drove by a Lexus car dealership, smiled, and thought rather easily, "The poetry I have on my front seat is worth so much more than the combined price of all those stunning cars." No poet, here or home, does so much with so little. The following tribute to Jesus moves us from talking about new life to feeling new hope:

> **spring song**
>
> *the green of Jesus*
> *is breaking the ground*
> *and the sweet*
> *smell of delicious Jesus*
> *is opening the house and*

> *the dance of Jesus music*
> *has hold of the air and*
> *the world is turning*
> *in the body of Jesus and*
> *the future is possible*
> (*The Collected Poems of Lucille Clifton 1965–2010*, ed. Kevin Young and Michael S. Glaser [Rochester: BOA Editions, 2012], 126)

Wonder on wonder and treat on treat, sometimes on the backside of poetry, a poem wells up inside me. As a matter of fanciful fact, it just happened as I concluded this section of the book. Honoring the timing, I am compelled to share with you what just arrived in my spirit. It makes me think of the ways stillness and joy are directly related and connected in ways I've never contemplated until now:

> ### The Great Secret
>
> *The great secret is this:*
> *In the back-room of*
> *stillness and silence,*
> *there is a loud party going on.*
>
> *God and all God's Children*
> *are singing and dancing*
> *and glad commotion of communion*
> *never ends.*
> —KBJ

Ironically, I sense that I can't say enough about the power of poetry, that which can say so much by saying so little. If you think my estimation of poetry to be excessive, hear the following words from Natasha Trethewey, current US Poet Laureate:

Poetry makes us more observant, more compassionate, empathetic. [It] is our best means of communicating with each other, of touching not only the intellect but the heart. [It] is the best repository for our most humane, ethical and just feelings. We can be made to experience the world, interior lives of other human beings, by reading poetry. (Mary Loftus, "Her Calling," *Emory Magazine*, Autumn 2012, 25)

If Trethewey is even close to being correct, those who would lead ought to think twice before going forth verseless. Speaking of verses, come to think of it, some of my favorite Scriptures are prose gone poetry:

"The Lord is my shepherd, I shall not want. . . ."

"The Lord is my strength and my salvation. . . ."

"I waited patiently on the Lord, and he inclined unto me and heard my cry."

"They that wait on the Lord shall renew their strength. They shall mount up with wings as eagles. . . ."

"Ye must be born again."

"Ye are the light of the world and the salt of the earth."

"What shall separate us from the love of God. . . ."

"And God shall wipe away all tears."

The power of these texts is not just in their declaration; it's in their formulation—it's in the music!

CHAPTER THREE

{ HOW STILLNESS ENHANCES LEADERSHIP }

*In a world of chronic activity, stillness and solitude
may seem deathly. Yet, the soul renewal of retreat
can inspire an aliveness we've never known before.*
—KBJ

The Silent Rock: Seven Concrete Ways Stillness Can Benefit Your Ministry

Perhaps the most important question a pulpit search committee could ever ask a potential pastoral candidate rarely is asked: How often and well do you practice stillness? Given our culture's linking of busyness with productivity and long-standing suspicion of idleness—we know whose workshop that is—the absence of such a question is understandable. Yet the absence of the stillness question should no longer be acceptable in a time of desperate need for ministers with unusual energy and imaginative insight in an ever-changing and complex world that often feels overwhelming.

I experience stillness as conscious and intentional moments of mental and emotional emptying and in-filling. Its effect is that it softens and opens me, making me feel like I have more space inside to be curious, think, create, risk, and change. That being said, rather than experiencing stillness as an addendum or obstruction to ministry, stillness has become, for me, a concrete ministry essential.

If Jesus is our "Solid Rock," as the hymn of my youth suggests, stillness is our "Silent Rock." Consider the following seven benefits of stillness to imagining and sustaining a fulfilling ministry in a demanding world:

1. *Ready curiosity as opposed to apprehension before the unfamiliar.* The unsung antidote for fear is curiosity. Become more interested in that which feels like a threat to you. Try as we may, we cannot rid ourselves of it: the goal of ministry is transformation, changed persons, changed groups, and a changed world. Transformation is dating the unfamiliar over and over again. Most of us prefer what we know to what we don't know, so there is a need to intentionally grow our capacity to willingly engage the unknown and to gently but effectively urge others to do the same. Stillness, engaging the mystery of nothingness, is a way to become regularly acquainted with and interested in the unfamiliar. As a leader's comfort with the unfamiliar grows, it may contribute to an organization more ready to engage as opposed to reject change. This welcoming energy related to the unfamiliar, including novel initiatives and programs, is more easily cycled into passionate enthusiasm for new church initiatives, especially ones that seek to replace deeply cherished and entrenched traditions.

2. *Peace rather than overanxiousness with conflict and paradox.* There is no progress without tension, and some of the richest truths are often paradoxes. Take, for instance, loving

one's enemy as a serious strategy for social change. The earliest followers of Jesus soon discovered that life loyal to Him meant coming into situations of conflict and competing desires and dreams. See Peter's interview on the night Jesus was captured. There is no management of the challenges of conflict, tension, and paradox, so vitally necessary for genuine growth, without inner peace to sustain us and help us to persevere. Without peace to firm us up, we may move swiftly to avoiding or suppressing tensions that are vital for personal and organizational progress.

Enter stillness. Stillness mediates peace inside of us. In stillness, we can bid tensions to be at bay as we soak our souls in the restorative and reassuring waters of God's love. Fully renewed, we may reengage in the sure knowledge that through it all, the most powerful reality of all is God's love and the peace it brings. Regulated on, in, and by peace, it is well. Through regular times of stillness, we may experience one of the greatest truths: if you can hold God's peace, you can hold anything. Such peace provides strength to negotiate, instead of avoiding or suppressing, creative tension and paradox. I'll say more about holding and honoring tension in a moment.

3. *Trust of vulnerability rather than defensiveness before challenge.* In stillness, our usual instruments of reasoning and verbalizing are temporarily limited and restricted. This leaves us open, and therefore vulnerable, to being acted upon without choosing to defend ourselves. The check on defensiveness in stillness may spill over into our becoming less defensive of ourselves and our ideas and programs as leaders. Spending less time and energy defending, we are better able to attune with persons. Attunement, fully understanding others if not fully agreeing with them, is an essential strength for effective leadership. As we are better attuned to persons, we are better able to communicate and connect with persons.

29

4. *Acceptance of interruptions as invitations as opposed to intrusions.* Stillness is allowance for empty spaces. One of the reasons we may become upset by the slightest adjustment to plans is that our plans are so compact and rigid. All too often, we find ourselves trapped in the tyranny of trying to do too much too fast. As stillness conditions us to the sweetness of spaciousness, we are inspired to allow for more spaces and pauses in the natural ebb and flow of everyday living. A day with more spaces is a day that is more gracious to the unplanned and unexpected. Because of our compelling encounters with God in the empty spaces during open devotion, we know that God is no less God in our unplanned as God is in our plans. Gorgeous God and Glory are going on all the time.

5. *Practicing communication as open dialogue as opposed to closed monologue.* Stillness is less a time for speaking and more a time for listening. The exercise of stillness-listening can condition us toward a listening posture in all of our communication. Listening's importance to leadership is indispensable. Through listening, we are able to hear from others regarding who they are and what truly matters to them. Seeking to lead without such sacred data nullifies our ability to interpret spiritual truths and impart spiritual blessings in ways that are valid and meaningful. Moreover, listening is a creative must. What we need to fulfill God's vision has been distributed among us all. Not to listen is to disconnect ourselves from the creative energy and vision of God that God has uniquely placed in each of us. We must listen to be whole, to be full.

6. *Having more patience than angst with waiting.* Leadership in ministry involves much waiting. We wait for sermon ideas, for persons to respond in counseling sessions, for the right moment and the right word in visitations, for the right timing regarding presenting new ministry initiatives, for persons to volunteer for this or that important church leadership position,

and more. There is no genuine pastoral leadership without waiting. Stillness helps to make us comfortable with waiting. Girded up by the power of creative waiting evident in stillness, we learn not just to wait but to wait in contentment. And to choose to be content is not to choose to be complacent. It is to choose to be actively at peace, and thus more posed for creative power. There is abundant energy to be mined in patient peace. We may come to find through stillness that enthusiasm and patience share a secret bond. Genuine flourishing need not be rushed.

7. *Deeper awareness and acceptance of the soft, subtle expressions of the subconscious mind and the inspiration of the Holy Spirit.* My greatest mentor in stillness offers the following wisdom that I have taped to my home office desk: "There is something in every one of you that waits and listens for the sound of the genuine in yourself" (Dr. Howard Thurman's Baccalaureate Address at Spelman University, May 4, 1980, edited by Jo Moore Stewart for the *Spelman Messenger* 96, no. 4, [Summer 1980]).

Such advice is golden. Since Thurman's articulation, entire books have been written about noticing and attending to one's inner voice, sometimes referred to as inner wisdom or intuition. One of my favorites is *Listen: Trusting Your Inner Voice in Times of Crisis* by Lynn A. Robinson. She elaborates on what she calls "your inner source of wisdom":

> This wisdom doesn't come from your logical mind. It comes from a spiritual source that you may experience as an inner prompting, an inspiration, a gut feeling, a quickening, a knowing deep in your heart. It doesn't speak to you through a megaphone or in a loud voice. In fact, most often it communicates through the proverbial "still, quiet, inner voice." ([Guilford, CT: Globe Pequot Press, 2010], ix)

31

If each one of us has such a voice, why are so many of us at a loss for clarity and guidance? The simple but pervasive answer is that too many of us don't spend enough time getting to know our inner voice, a voice many of us took for granted when we were children. As adults, shouted down by the voices of others, our inner voice grows softer and softer. Glory of glories, because it is an expression of the Great Voice, your inner voice never goes completely silent. Because God is eternal, so are our inner voices. It is a voice that even death can't silence. I believe it to be that part of us, along with our souls, that never dies but returns more fully home to where it has resided all the time.

There is no greater calling in life than to get better at heeding the callings of our inner voice: the sacred voice of one's genuine sound. Being able to hear and heed that voice more clearly and convincingly strengthens us to seek and trust it more. If we want to know the real truth, Kabir invites us to "listen to the secret sound, the real sound, which is inside you."

There is your voice, and there is the Voice of the Holy Spirit.

I once received the following confession from a deeply committed young pastor making his way along the adventurous and treacherous terrain of his first church:

> As a young pastor, I am constantly wrestling with the dichotomy of showing confidence and poise before the people, while wondering internally if the direction and pace of my leadership are in line with God's will. Some days, I know what to do. Others, I am just not sure. Perhaps such is the delicate dance of those selected to hear the music of God's voice in leading His people. Fortunately, I have been blessed with spiritual choreographers who speak into my life at critical times, whose words always get me back in step.

This pastor's words capture the beauty and risks of leadership as well as any four sentences I've read on the matter. His use of the dance image, and the need to be brought again and again back in step, resonates with my more than four decades of experience in ministry. The great challenge of our busy times is not to be so busy as to miss hearing the rhythms of the Spirit. Dancing with a listening air is a skill to be developed and celebrated continually in ministry. With all due respect to knowledge, skills, methods, and strategies, it is the Spirit who gives life to ministry.

Listening for the rhythms of the Spirit in silence and stillness allows us to better distinguish and dance to them amid the many sounds and voices of ministry. As long as you can hear the Spirit, you can dance.

Space for Grace

In basketball, it is important to learn how to create space in order to get a shot off. Exceptional shooters are as adept at putting space between themselves and their defenders as they are at putting the ball in the net. Likewise, we can create space for allowing more grace to flow in our relationships.

For example, once after listening to someone express her hurt about having been wronged by a loved one, I asked her if she thought that her loved one would have knowingly hurt her so deeply. In other words, had she known that her words were going to wound as they did, would the loved one have uttered them? After an extended pause, I heard what sounded like an honest answer: "No." In an instant, the speaker's demeanor changed; I could sense her heart soften. The question had prompted a shift in perspective, which allowed for a more merciful interpretation of the situation. The question made room for space, and the space made room for grace.

Just a slight change in perspective can change our hearts and attitudes toward each other for the better. All we need do is take a moment to step back and ask a few questions, or maybe just one, and peace can once again reside in a relationship. Our attempting to see things from a different perspective is a way of making space for grace. And, glory to God, grace doesn't need a whole lot of space to make a real difference. Glory on glory, when it comes to God's grace, it's not about what we did or didn't do; it's about grace.

Holding and Honoring Creative Tension

Cultivate the ability to hold tension in life-giving ways.
—Parker J. Palmer

Gregg Levoy's *Callings: Finding and Following an Authentic Life* is a book as beautiful as it is profound. If not the entire book, his chapter "Braving Conflict" should be required reading for all who would lead. Levoy writes of the need to "embrace seemingly opposing forces without rejecting one or the other for the sheer relief of it." He admits that such a task is indeed a calling of callings:

> Sometimes these contrary exertions inside us feel like gladiators tied together for a fight to the finish, and sometimes like the swimming bodies of yin and yang swirling around in the same fishbowl. Either way, the opposing forces occupy a space that is like an ecotone, a transition zone between two ecological communities like forest and grassland or river and desert. They compete, yes; the word *ecotone* means a house divided, a system in tension. But they also exchange, swapping juices, information, and resources. Ecotones have tremendous biological diversity and resilience. ([New York: Three Rivers Press, 1997], 53)

Many pastoral leaders who are ordained, in part, to be practitioners and presenters of peace often have a blind spot when it comes to appreciating the reality and benefit of creative conflict. Equating success with the absence of conflict, we tend to be uncomfortable when persons are upset with each other. For the sake of peace, we seek to ease tensions and make people play nice again as quickly as possible. The hidden problem is that such tension-easing often prevents a congregation from undergoing the challenging, honest engagement it needs to have in order to change and grow. Genuine peace, as the understanding of *shalom* yields, is not simply the absence of conflict; it is the presence of wellness and wholeness. Wellness and wholeness are rarely attained by avoiding conflict and discomfort.

In his legendary "Letter from Birmingham Jail," referred to by S. Jonathan Bass as "The Prison Epistle," Martin Luther King Jr. reminds clergy concerned with heightened community tensions that tension, rather than being a dead-end street, was a passageway for growth:

> This may sound rather shocking. But I must confess that I am not afraid of the word "tension." I have earnestly worked and preached against violent tension, but there is a type of constructive, nonviolent tension that is necessary for growth.

What has stillness to do with this? Practicing stillness promotes waiting and holding without needing to move from the place of one's honest being at the time, including the being of being conflicted and feeling disrupted. Being able to sit privately with discomfort washes over into being able to sit with discomfort in difficult conversations and meetings without feeling led to douse flames of contention too quickly. In this sense, being a firefighter is not the first or highest calling of a leader. Leaders in love with growth need to be fire-holders, able to hold the flame of creative contention until persons are able to envision and feel the light and heat of holy transformation that it yields.

Tender Mending in Wordless Waiting

Hosting stillness regularly enables us to hold grief, our own and that of others, without running away.

Some of my saddest moments of all have occurred while serving as a pastoral leader. One such time was when I was asked to preside at a funeral for a youngster, about three or four years old, who had choked to death on a piece of a sausage. The grief was oh so hard. The longest ride of my life was to the cemetery that day, sitting silent in the front passenger seat. Behind us, though it seems too sad to be true to me now, sat the parents, the father holding the small casket of his son gone too soon.

Then there was precious Keshana Lathem, a princess of a child killed at the age of six one Saturday night. She fell prey to a bullet shot through the front door of her home. As she was a member of our Sunday school, I visited Keshana's family early the next awful morning. All were still in shock, most of all Keshana's broken young mother, who lay in bed sobbing and weeping, and cradling a framed portrait of her baby so brutally taken from her hours before.

In both these midnight moments, words were too much and too little. What was needed was a sacred non-saying, a witness that was helplessness but not just that: helplessness surrounded by soft spaciousness sufficient enough to cushion grief with unspeakable mercy.

Ministerial leaders are potentially strongest in moments of human brokenness and despair, including our own, when we are able to be fully present without feeling the need to present.

Sacred non-presenting holds and honors space for a Presence of Healing Love able to sustain one and all when we are wounded to soul's core.

It is stillness that most honestly reflects and respects the helplessness we feel when our hearts are broken. Through stillness, we have room to hurt as much as we want and need without being stopped or judged. Through stillness, we have space and place to lodge quiet and not-so-quiet indictments against a God who at times appears to be so Godless. Through stillness, horror has a chance at being fully owned, if never fully understood.

The hushed unrushed miracle is that the hard owning of grief is hospitable to healing. And even if the grief never goes away for good, we are blessed, in time and mercy, to be able to make room for other things. "There is a balm in Gilead to make the wounded whole," the Negro spiritual repeats from scripture. Nothing more need be said or repeated. The only necessary grace amid grief is provided for even before vicious blow: tender mending in wordless waiting.

Space for Reflective Noticing

Stillness increases our capacity to create spaces in our busy lives with confidence and comfort. The result is life enrichment when it comes to realities we often don't notice as much as we should. Noticing them more allows us to learn lessons, make connections, and cultivate deeper, more compelling meaning for our existence. I am convinced that the following reflection on Rosa Parks would not have been possible apart from taking time and space to notice and reflect.

We Are Rosa Parks

Where were you when you heard that Rosa Parks had died? What were you doing? How did you respond to the news?

Though I had not spoken her name or thought about her recently, I found myself momentarily numbed by the news of her passing. It was as if something precious beyond comprehension had left our world, had left me. So, I stopped what I was doing and just sat. We rush everything these days, including our grieving. Let us resist moving past the death of Rosa Parks too swiftly. In tribute to one whose sitting changed a nation, we do well to sit and think.

In her book *Black Womanist Ethics*, Katie Cannon writes about "unshouted courage," calling it "the quality of steadfastness, akin to fortitude, in the face of formidable oppression" ([Atlanta: Scholars Press, 1988], 144). Rosa Parks personified "unshouted courage" in her unpretentious act of civil disobedience on a Montgomery bus over fifty years ago and the calm, though deliberate, manner in which she recalled her act in countless interviews thereafter. What a stunning contrast to Martin Luther King Jr.'s and Malcolm X's volcanic vocal pronouncements. Rosa Parks reminds us that courage comes in many shapes, sizes, and voices, even a voice just above a whisper. The question is not will you or I be courageous like Rosa Parks or any of the sung and unsung champions of the civil rights movement, but will we be true to our convictions in ways that are true to who we are? Will I listen to and own my unique courageous voice? Will you?

I cannot think of Rosa Parks without recalling some of the most profound words I have read concerning her. In *Let Your Life Speak*, Parker Palmer interprets Parks's protest as an action whereby she affirmed personal wholeness: she refused to think free and act oppressed:

> Where do people find the courage to live divided no more when they know they will be punished for it? They have come to understand that no punishment anyone might inflict on them could possibly be worse than the

punishment they inflict on themselves by conspiring in their own diminishment. ([San Francisco: Jossey-Bass, 2000], 34)

We conspire in our own diminishment each time we act contrary to our most honorable and liberating beliefs. We are Rosa Parks each time we have the heart to reject that which holds us down and reach for that which urges us on. Rosa Parks did not have a monopoly on living with integrity; we can do so each day in our aspirations, relationships, and decisions.

Early in her writing career, Alice Walker was asked by a leading national magazine to write about growing up in the South. Though Walker was pleased with what she produced, the magazine suggested major revisions. Walker refused. In a showdown meeting, Walker was informed that she didn't understand—the piece would have to be changed or it would not be published. After considering the positive impact such an article would have on her budding career and weighing that against her integrity as a writer, Walker responded, "It's you who do not understand. All I have to do in life is save my soul." Rosa Parks's decision was a matter of soul-saving, her own and that of a nation.

Now, we must be careful that we do not do with Rosa Parks what we do with many of our heroes. We tend to place laudable figures so high on the pedestal of praise that they become untouchable, out of living range. The lessons of Rosa Parks are much too valuable to be stored away in history books and museums. We need her beacon light witness of personal uniqueness and wholeness nearby to behold and manifest in everyday life. In this way, Rosa Parks will not simply be a wondrous woman of sainted dignity and sacred defiance who lived once, but a spirit of freedom, justice, and personal integrity who lives now in each of us.

Living Graced Up: Facing God's Difficult Children

I remember driving to the church in angst. I was scheduled to meet with a church leader who seemed committed to combat. He was known throughout the church for his behavior but was rarely called on it due to "his service to the church." Does this sound familiar? Though I'd been at the church a short time, I'd already seen his diminishing demeanor on display. Yet, having just arrived, I'd also been the recipient of his seemingly honest and sincere goodwill and hospitality. While I drove to the church, my angst was mostly triggered by my sensing that I'd be arriving a few minutes late. I wondered about the impression of me he'd have as a result. I began to posture myself for a ready defense if I were attacked in any way regarding my commitment to time management or lack thereof. Then grace came. I took a few deep breaths and began to speak wholesome affirmations to myself. Next, I envisioned a spirit of grace surrounding us both. Both practices, affirmations and envisioning persons surrounded by the light of grace, are daily spiritual rituals. Basically, I was drawing from my well of morning grace to grace myself and the church leader. The meeting went off without incident, which for pastors means without overt criticism.

I don't mean to suggest that all we have to do to remedy strained and potentially toxic relationships in churches is to say and see better. Certain situations call for professional input. Moreover, separation and termination are sometimes the holiest of actions. Yet, in a great many situations, the way toward more harmonious existence is the way of greater grace.

Allow me this risky oversimplification: graced people grace people. Hurting people hurt people. Where there is hurt, there is for sure a need for more grace. We cannot give what we don't have. Stillness is a time of grace in-filling. We can never hold too much grace, and there is always more grace where grace comes from. It is possible to leave such moments so filled with grace that it conditions our self-esteem to be less worried about what others think if we fail to measure up in this or that way. Though we live as responsibly as we can, our sense of self-worth is not so easily threatened. We are confident souls, gracely rooted in God's unconditional love. To be rooted in grace is to live graced up. Such a sanctified state allows for having grace and more grace at the ready to engage others in healthy, wholesome, and responsible ways, including and especially the most difficult of God's children.

P.S. Two affirmations for the road:

I am a confident, creative soul, gracely rooted in God's unconditional love.

I relax and revel in knowing that there is always more grace where grace comes from.

Waiting for the Sermon

The stillness muscle properly exercised in one's personal devotional life may significantly help preaching. An unsung sermon preparation skill is the ability to sit with the text and allow questions to surface, observations to arise, and the unsaid to declare itself. Waiting in stillness is essential not only to catching relevant and meaningful sermon ideas, but also to presenting those ideas in ways that stick in the listener's head and heart. There is nothing more tragic than a worthy idea expressed poorly. Often, sermons come across less effectively than possible because preachers simply have not taken the time to listen for just the right words. Mark Twain remarked, "The difference between the right word and the almost right word is the difference between lightning and the lightning bug."

The most important factor in a preacher's ability to say may be her ability to *not say*. The truly liberating word hinges on fearlessness before wordlessness, on trust in silence. Esteemed spiritual sage Abraham Heschel whispers, "The strength of faith is in silence, in words that hibernate and wait. Uttered faith must come out as surplus of silence, as the fruit of lived faith, of enduring intimacy" (*Moral Grandeur and Spiritual Audacity: Abraham Joshua Heschel, Essays,* ed. Susannah Heschel [New York: Farrar, Straus, and Giroux, 1996], 264). It is wordsmith Frederick Buechner who reminds us that "before the Gospel is a word, it is silence" (*Telling the Truth: The Gospel as Tragedy, Comedy, and Fairy Tale* [New York: Harper & Row, 1977], 25).

Poetry on Stillness

Where Love Lives

If you can be

still enough

long enough

there is a place within

on the other side of silence

where love lives.

—KBJ

Lounging in God's Grace

God, help me to be still

to lounge

in Your grace

and listen

to Your song,

and to hear my song

in Yours.

—KBJ

The Best Voyage of All

There are

few voyages

more adventurous

or enriching

than the ones

that take place

in still waters.

—KBJ

Unsung Thrill

The most exciting thing

in the world

that we can never do enough

is sit still in

God's warm and gentle grace.

It is while basking in the

sunshine of God's grace

that we can be thrilled

deep down within by

just being alive in love:

That surprise

of surprises

we didn't earn,

don't deserve

and never saw coming.

—KBJ

The Daily Baptism

Wading through

Stillness

We are baptized

Afresh

In the

Washing

Waters of

Shalom.

—KBJ

{ OBSERVING AWARENESS }

As he thinks in his heart, so is he.
—Proverbs 23:7 (NKJV)

Most people come to know only one corner of their room,
one spot near the window, one narrow strip on which
they keep walking back and forth.
—Rainer Maria Rilke, Letters to a Young Poet

These losses are necessary because we grow
by losing and leaving and letting go.
—Judith Viorst, Necessary Losses

The Incarnation: God's Way of Saving and Savoring Life

It does not surprise me that our son, Jared, a young man now with a beautiful family, is a morning person. He always has been. As a matter of fact, at one point he was such a morning person that he wanted everyone in the house to know about it. When he was about two or three, Jared went through a period of announcing his arrival to the day. On some days, we would hear his public cry much earlier than we desired. From his room, he yelled at the top of his voice, "I waked up!" It went on like that for several weeks. I remember suggesting to my wife that we have him examined to see if this strange behavior was normal. Indeed, as I reflected on his morning declaration years later, I came to understand that his behavior was beyond normal; it was magnificent. Being awake, aware of, and appreciative of the new day was somehow deeply thrilling for our son. Such a thing is itself thrilling and divine.

Is there any greater witness to the spirituality of being fully awake to life than the Incarnation? God in Christ is God being so excited about the reality of human existence that God can't help but become human Godself. What if God didn't become human just to save life, but to savor life?

Think about it. In God in Christ Jesus, we have one who is so interested in knowledge that as a boy, he lags behind in Jerusalem to learn more; one so interested in socializing that he begins his ministry at a wedding feast; one so interested in the hurting that he becomes a healer; one so interested in nature that he uses the ordinary around people, like the lilies of the field, to explode the extraordinary inside of people; one so interested in continuing a friendship that he raises Lazarus; one so interested in keeping in touch after he's gone that he offers a lasting memorial of his body and blood; and one so taken with being alive that he refuses to remain dead.

Because Jesus savored life so, he was able to discern how life could be appropriated to enjoy and explain God's love. Savoring life is a grand unsung reservoir of vitality for creative and meaningful ministry.

The first lines of Robinson Jeffers's soulful poem "Return" come to mind:

> *A little too abstract, a little too wise,*
> *It is time for us to kiss the earth again,*
> (*The Selected Poetry of Robinson Jeffers,* ed. Tim Hunt
> [Palo Alto: Stanford University Press, 2002], 499)

There is no vibrant ministry apart from our letting the rich life, by living with incarnational savoring awareness, run through our roots again, and again, and again.

Waking Up: The Call of Awareness

The following paragraph from *Awareness* by Anthony de Mello remains one of the most meaningful processions of words I have ever come upon, and they have never stopped marching in my mind:

> Spirituality means waking up. Most people, even though they don't know it, are asleep. They're born asleep, they live asleep, they marry in their sleep, they breed children in their sleep, they die in their sleep without ever waking up. They never understand the loveliness and the beauty of this thing that we call human existence. (*Awareness* [New York, Doubleday, 1990], 5)

Why did these words stun me so and stay with me? Perhaps because they presented a novel understanding of spirituality to me, one that challenged and expanded previous notions of spirituality. I believe I grew up thinking that though there was a cognitive dimension to spirituality, it was subjugated to a spiritual dimension. de Mello's presentation seemed to prioritize the cognitive as much as it did the spiritual. First, spirituality is not just a change of heart; it is a change of mind—a mind-waker and mind-opener. Second, this understanding of spirituality as a wake-up call of sorts was not just coming to a greater awareness of one's spiritual nature but arriving at a deeper appreciation for human existence. Life is not something merely to be tolerated on the way to eternity; life is a magnificent gift to be celebrated and savored. One does not get to God around life; one perceives God through life. There is no authentic spirituality to be derived from going around life. de Mello's words suggest that spirituality and living awareness and appreciation are one and the same.

The Deeper Awareness

We often just taste the top of a blessing. Go deeper, and we find wonder under wonder.

There is a story told of the musk deer of north India. In the springtime, the roe is haunted by the odor of musk. He runs wildly over hill and ravine with his nostrils dilating and his little body throbbing with desire, sure that around the next clump of trees or bush he will find musk, the object of his quest. Then at last he falls, exhausted, with his little head resting on his tiny hoofs, only to discover that the odor of musk is in his own hide.

So often, the musk deer's fate is our own. We push and pull so hard so often to be acknowledged and affirmed. This inner drive to be accepted can get out of hand when the acceptance is not easily won, and we end up overreaching for it in our relationships and our jobs. Additionally, many of us know that the acceptance feeling tends to wear off pretty quickly when it is overlinked to achievement and accomplishment. Almost immediately, we begin to desire a higher degree of acceptance associated with a higher level of achievement. The result is the maddening tyranny of never feeling fully satisfied.

Thankfully, there is a clear way out of such a predicament. That way is living FROM acceptance, not FOR acceptance. Grace is the difference between living from acceptance and for acceptance. Living from acceptance is living with the firm belief that you are eternally embraced in the most exquisite love of all, God's love. Most important, such glorious internal acceptance is not based on what you do, but who you are. God's love is all encompassing and all fulfilling. We are the created love children of God, conceived and created by love, for love. Wonder on wonder: the Giver is also Gift, and the Gift is within. Living with the glad awareness of God's love within eliminates the need to overreach for acceptance elsewhere, ever again. That living truth has the power to transform leading from a push-and-pull affair into a grace-and-give affair. The result may be the daunting pleasure of getting used to ministry in a spirit of unrelenting lightness of heart.

From Grace to Great

The Japanese artist Katsushika Hokusai is perhaps best known as author of the woodblock print series *Thirty-Six Views of Mount Fuji*, which includes the internationally recognized print *The Great Wave of Kanagawa*, created during the 1820s, when Hokusai was in his sixties. In his seventies, Hokusai produced another significant landscape series, *One Hundred Views of Mount Fuji*. In the postscript to this work, the artist wrote,

> From around the age of six, I had the habit of sketching from life. I became an artist, and from fifty on began producing works that won some reputation, but nothing I did before the age of seventy was worthy of attention. At seventy-three, I began to grasp the structures of birds and beasts, insects and fish, and of the way plants grow. If I go on trying, I will surely understand them still better by the time I am eighty-six, so that by ninety, I will have penetrated to their essential nature. At one hundred, I may well have a

positively divine understanding of them, while at one hundred and thirty, forty, or more I will have reached the stage where every dot and every stroke I paint will be alive. May Heaven, that grants long life, give me the chance to prove that this is no lie. (Robert Fulghum, *Words I Wish I Wrote* [New York: HarperPerennial, 1999], 55)

Awareness is not just about being more keenly aware of what is; it is about being more keenly aware of what can be and what is made more possible through sustained visionary imagining. Great leaders have great visions, beginning with how they envision their own continued being and becoming in the world.

Leaders are persons first. Who you see yourself to be as a person has direct impact on your effectiveness as a leader. For example, Martin Luther King Jr.'s ability to imagine an alternative world devoid of racism, militarism, and economic disparity was, I believe, rooted in his settled and affirming sense of self. Though he was reared in the cruelly segregated South, his esteem was strengthened from the beginning by loving family members and the spiritually and emotionally rich ground of Ebenezer Baptist Church. His self-esteem firmly rooted, the young aspiring minister was free and fierce enough to reach beyond the familiar setting of home to a wider world he felt comfortable traversing and engaging. His ability to be at home with himself allowed him to be at home in the larger world and subsequently to imagine and labor toward a new world order. Healthy self-awareness is creatively energizing. Freed from draining emotional toiling within, we are able to spend more energy genuinely flourishing. Knowing who we are frees us to be more fully who we are in unusually meaningful and powerful ways. In regard to leadership, the most obvious impact of self-esteem is the cultivation of an indispensable leadership quality: confidence.

What is your self-perception? Whom do you see yourself becoming? What do you celebrate about yourself? Have you fully accepted who you are? How do you imagine the answers to such questions having implications for your role as a leader?

Claiming and Crafting Your Inner Wisdom

Though we are created human beings by God, our becoming as human beings is an act of co-creation involving God, others, and ourselves. Several years ago, I began to wonder if there was a way I could become more helpful in the process. How could I contribute to my own development as a person, and thus as a leader, more deliberately and intentionally? I realized that one of the first things I needed to do was excavate my most impactful beliefs. By impactful, I mean the beliefs that I actually allowed to be alive inside me to form and frame my journey in the world.

What were the ideas that mattered most to me and influenced me the most from day to day? I spent hours listening for my most precious truths, paying close attention to those sentiments that seemed to repeat themselves in my head and heart.

My hopeful suspicion was that if I could name my most cherished beliefs, I could lean into them more, understanding how and why they were benefitting me as a person and pastor. With this understanding, I could build personal rituals and practices that would inspire personal and professional growth.

What finally formed for me were seven values that I framed into affirmations for ready claiming and more intentional exercising in my life on a regular basis. Below are the Sacred Seven. They are seven truths with corresponding descriptive sentences that help set my internal mental thermostat each morning and several times a day. Repeating them helps to energize me for living and flourishing in the world. Given the constant bombardment of information—good, bad, and in between—it is so easy to be bowled over by negativism and dimmed aspiration. The Sacred Seven keep me grounded in love and inspired for continual exploration and expansion. Such a goal on my part is less inspired by the gurus of positive thinking and New Age skywalkers, and more by the vision of Jesus who came that we might have life and "have it more abundantly" (John 10:10, NKJV). Repeating the Sacred Seven is my mental strategy for intentionally staying in Abundant Life Mode:

1. *I Am a Child of God.* We are continually loved from the inside out and from the outside in by a God of relentless grace and mercy.

2. *I play and soar in the Spirit.* We are called to delight and aspire in God, even as God delights and aspires in us.

3. *I co-create my life with my thoughts and deeds.* Life is God's gift to us; how we choose to live life is our gift to God.

4. *I explore and expand daily.* We are constantly thrilled and rethrilled by "the divine next" in life.

5. *I join others in creating the Beloved Community.* Every person is a unique expression of God, having a priceless offering for God's world.

6. *I practice enlightened perseverance.* We keep on keeping on, ever learning, seeking, and finding as we go.

7. *It is well with my soul.* Chronic stress is not mandatory; we have a holy right to peace of mind, heart, and soul.

I have discovered these Sacred Seven daily declarations to be especially powerful for building three crucial dimensions of inner strength: Imagination, Confidence, and Perseverance.

Imagination is, I believe, the second most powerful force in life, second only to love. Imagination is our ability to dream. It is through dreaming that we envision such wondrous realities as more abundant living, resilience through adversity, and fabulous new adventures and discoveries that challenge and grow us to heights seen and unseen. Without imagining, life is stripped of its heights. With imagination, all things are possible, and we are inspired to soar.

Confidence is the strength to trust what we imagine. My mightiest mentor in this regard is my mother, Ora Mae Jones. Though she is deceased, I speak of her in the present tense because I can yet hear her, at times stronger than ever before, encouraging me to "just be positive and stay confident." Mama didn't just encourage confidence; she lived confidence. There was a sense of sacred boldness about her that insisted she could face anything. To this day, I marvel at her inner resolve, determination, and confidence.

Perseverance is the power to keep on keeping on. Even the brightest imagination and the toughest confidence are tested and tried by adversity and challenge. No one is exempted from suffering. No one escapes heartache. Yet there are countless testimonies of persons the world over who have survived and even thrived while bearing unspeakable burdens. Their common characteristic is perseverance, inspired by an Unseen Bearer of Burden-Bearers. While facing immeasurable hardship, such persons have had a way of hearing an Unusual Calming Whisper saying, "You are not alone. I am with you. Together, we will make it through."

For more information about my seven life-changing awareness affirmations, see *The Sacred Seven: How to Create, Manage, and Sustain a Fulfilling Life*, a small book written not just for clergy and leaders, but for all seeking an enhanced vision of optimal spiritual living amid everyday challenges.

The Best Soul Wisdom of All

I have been trumpeting awareness in this chapter as not just our knowing apparatus, but our knowing holdings: wisdom we know to be most true that is of greatest value to us as persons and leaders. This is formative awareness and wisdom. Perhaps the greatest word of wisdom is what I now share with you. I believe the following truth to be a matter of soul wisdom: it is something we know in our deepest being, but somehow we have forgotten or live as if we have. Reminders come through grace. Such a grace moment happened one Wednesday morning, January 5, 2011.

During my early morning devotional, I began to hear sentences in my mind. This was not strange. As a preacher and writer, I am always hearing sentences, phrases, words that bid me, somehow, to go seeking after them. But there was something different about what I heard that morning. There was a clarity that was fearlessly striking. Though I did not hear an audible voice, the words seemed to sound in my mind and spirit with the effect of an audible voice. One sentence came after another. Feeling increasingly emotional, to the point of tearing up, I began writing down the strange but deeply compelling procession of words. It was not until the moment was over and I started reviewing what I had written that I noticed the sentences were connected and capable of making me feel God's love in a refreshing new way. I call what I heard and took into my heart that morning a Love Letter from God:

Dear Child,

I love you for you. Let go, and let yourself feel loved. All the love you deserve and thought you never had is yours right now. But you must let me love you. All the sunshine in the world means nothing, if you won't see the light or feel the warmth.

Letting yourself feel my love changes everything. Let me love you, and then you live my love.
    Love you madly, always have and always will,
God

The most precious soul wisdom of all is that we are the Beloved of God. We are continually being loved from the inside out and the outside in by a God of relentless grace and mercy. The sweetest decision in all the world is to choose to accept our divine acceptance and proceed to live from acceptance and not for acceptance. This sweetest decision in all the world can make all the difference in the world.

Because we are always in love and love is always in us, the spiritual journey may be interpreted as an adventurous pilgrimage toward more deliberate and sustained awareness and acceptance of God's love. We may also speak of this process or transformation as remembering that we are loved. With this in mind, I offer the following "remembrance strategies" for your consideration:

1. *Notice God's Love More.* God shows signs of magnificent affection through persons, nature, and situations all the time. Slow down, pay attention, and savor life, God's love gift, more.

2. *Visualize Receiving God's Love.* Be still and relax your mind. Once you feel relaxed enough, envision yourself being loved by God in meaningful ways. Here are some possibilities: (a) See yourself being refreshed beneath the majestic waterfall of God's love. (b) Take an imaginative swim in the invigorating ocean of God's love. (c) Relax all the tension in your body as you let God hug and hold you. We hug God by being who we are. (For a touching example of receiving and resting in love, see John 12:1-3.)

3. *Affirm God's Love.* Words and beliefs are significant building blocks we use to help construct our living reality every day.

Affirmations are worded beliefs that we can either say aloud or utter silently to remind us of God's dynamic love. Here are three of my favorite affirmations that always soothe my soul with a refreshing sense of God's love:

"Good Morning, Child of God."

"I relax free and easy in God's free and easy grace."

"What's in me is greater than what's against me."

May you remember and keep remembering that you are the Beloved of God, to the point that this best truth of all becomes not just second nature to you, but first and final nature.

CHAPTER FIVE

{ LIVING AWARENESS }

*One of the best things about living is being
unexpectedly moved by the
unexplainable charm of life itself.*
—KBJ

Mining the Morning Mind

The biblical poet-king, David, once proclaimed, "Weeping may endure for a night, / But joy comes in the morning" (Psalm 30:5, NKJV). As it turns out, the morning may have more visitors than just joy. As we awaken with fresh energy and renewed enthusiasm, early day provides a spacious playground for creative and meaningful inspiration and reflection. Here are a few suggestions for uncovering the precious offerings of the morning mind.

1. *Remember and Reflect on Your Dreams.* Because our minds are less restricted and inhibited when we are at rest, our dreams are a rich resource of wisdom and guidance. But dreams are, as well, amazingly slippery. They can escape from our mental grasp in an instant. Now you see them; now you don't. In order to hold on to as much dream wisdom as possible, make dream

reflection an early-morning priority. Don't even wait until you arrive at your home office desk; keep a notebook near your bedside so that you are able to capture dreams and their messages first thing in the morning.

2. *Note New Road Signs.* One of the amazing wonders of humanness is that our minds may engage challenging problems while we are sleeping. Though at rest, mentally we are very much alive, perhaps in ways that we cannot be during our waking moments. The benefit of this is to have placed before us as we arise solutions to perplexing problems that seemed insolvable before we retired for the evening. Take some moments during your early time to read, record, and be grateful for the road signs offering guidance and direction, mysteriously and graciously constructed while you were asleep.

3. *Create New Options.* The early-morning mind has the luxury of not having been barnstormed by the demands, pressures, and worries of the day. Such early-morning spaciousness should not be wasted. While you are still free to think more of what you want to think and have the fresh energy to do so, nudge yourself to discover and create new ideas and possibilities. One of the best ways to begin doing this is by asking different questions. Ask away in a spirit of curiosity gone wild. Revel in the liberating truth that your only limitation, especially in the morning, is your own imagination.

Being Aware of Being Accepted

I doubt if we ever live beyond the possibility of being disappointed. If we live long enough, it's possible to identify those things that have a way of disappointing us the most. For me, one such disappointment is feeling let down by an inspired idea that seemed to hold mammoth potential. How is it possible that something you have such wonderful feelings about can seem to crash and burn so soon after burning strong inside of you?

I was in the grasp of such a disappointment one morning, yet I persisted in limping my way through a time of morning devotion. It was toward the end of my devotion that I began to feel a softening of my spirit and my limping being transformed into a new step. Soon after, the following words held me:

> There is a peace that does not depend on how we may feel or what we may have accomplished. It is derived from being aware of being accepted by God.

As the grace of these words held and hugged me, I began holding and hugging back. When all others have stopped, God is still applauding you.

There are entirely too many twists and turns in life to link our sense of well-being to circumstances. Thankfully, there is an oh-so-sweet alternative: rooting our wellness in the wellspring of God's unconditional grace and mercy.

The gift to leadership from our allowing ourselves to accept our acceptance is self-surrendering, an unspoken necessary action of leadership. It is the necessary vulnerability without which we can never realize our full potential as leaders. In his soulful book *The Inner Voice of Love*, Henri Nouwen offers the following testimony:

> Only when you know yourself as unconditionally loved— that is, fully received—by God can you give gratuitously. Giving without wanting anything in return is trusting that all your needs will be provided for by the One who loves you unconditionally. . . . You cannot give yourself to others if you do not own yourself, and you can only truly own yourself when you have been fully received in unconditional love. ([New York: Doubleday, 1996], 65)

The Fourth Response: Continually Inspired by God's Love

Before a world as complex and ever-changing as ours, the preferred options seem to be: (1) Be numb to it all. (2) Be burned out by it all. (3) Barely make it from day to day. There is another alternative, a fourth response: thrive in the midst of it all in who we are and what we do. That is not to say we will not have our days when the prior three options will have their way with us. But it is to say that it is possible to imagine being continually fulfilled sufficient enough to offer creative leadership even, dare I say especially, in the midst of trying times.

The doorway to this fourth response is daring to believe that there has been and always will be a Mighty Presence in the world even more powerful than the worst crisis. This is a Love as relentless as the world can sometimes feel heartless. This is the power of God's relentless love.

Such a love is not to be relegated to the realm of many-splendored things having no practical meaning for daily living and leading. Love of God creates limitless aspiration. Love of self cultivates confidence. Love of others nurtures compassion. Limitless aspiration, confidence, and compassion are fundamental strengths of a strong leader.

Say a fourth response to a daunting world is possible. How do we continually perceive and appropriate such energizing and creative divine love?

One way is to spot it and celebrate it. Mind you, because God is everywhere, the so-called sacred has no monopoly on the witness of God's love. God's love may be enjoyed, experienced, and appropriated anywhere and at any time. Madeleine L'Engle once said, "There is nothing so secular that it cannot be sacred" (*Walking on Water*, Harold Shaw Publishers, 1980).

I contend that God is as much God in the mud as God is God in the rainbow. Speaking of muddy rainbows . . .

Finding God's Love in Jazz

I want to mentally bow in reverence sometimes when I say the names Ella Fitzgerald and Louis Armstrong—perhaps the two most beloved persons in the history of jazz. Their magnificent power transcends their mesmerizing artistry. Their continuing bright witness in the world has to do with the world of lavish divine affection inside each of them. When they sing and play, it's as if Someone Greater is at work singing and playing inside of them.

I have felt this firsthand. Some years ago, I was having a tough Saturday night. It had been a trying week, and I didn't have a clue about what I would be preaching the next day. As an escape from the fatigue of ministry and the burden of preaching preparation, I decided to listen to music, but not my traditional Saturday evening gospel inspiration. Instead, perhaps as an act of defiance, I began listening to Ella Fitzgerald. As she sang, something happened that was totally unexpected. I began to feel that Ella Fitzgerald was singing directly to me. Her angelic voice was simultaneously soft and piercing. This amazing voice and the meaningful lyrics of songs like "I Cried for You," "My Melancholy Baby," and "Reach for Tomorrow" touched my heart and renewed my spirit. And wonder of wonders, I found myself ministering with fresh joy on Sunday morning.

That Saturday night was one of the most deeply spiritual moments of my life. Though no God or Jesus or anything biblical was in any of the song lyrics, I felt God in the room and in my heart. *God need not be named to be known.*

As for Armstrong, I begin my Jazz of Preaching class with a viewing of an enthralling performance by him at the Newport Jazz Festival in 1970. (The entire concert, including many jazz greats and Mahalia Jackson and Louis Armstrong joining flames on "Just a Closer Walk with Thee," is available on the DVD *Louis Armstrong: Good Evening Ev'rybody.*) He is ailing and has been advised not to blow his horn, so he just sings. His just singing his theme song, "When It's Sleepy Time Down South," is as good a picture as I have ever seen, and suspect will ever see, of one truly filled with the Holy Spirit.

When I hear both Armstrong and Fitzgerald, my sense is that I am hearing a Spirit within their spirits. It is a Spirit of generous loving acceptance and joy running over.

The Power of the Beloved Mind for Leadership

Awareness of God's love is a gigantic key to unleashing great wisdom, peace, and joy. The loving mind is a supple mind. At ease with itself, not looking to attack or defend, the loving mind is free to engage itself with what is and to dance with varied and sundry options in regard to what might be. The loving mind, because it is so lavishly non-judgmental, is always open to more choices, options, and possibilities. A loving mind is a prime instrument for a creative leader.

The ripple effect of a beloved mind is inner peace. Much of the emotional disorientation that we feel is a result of our minds being tossed about by this worry and that fear. The loving mind regularly soaked in the unconditional grace of God is galvanized for peace. It knows what it feels like to have the prayer "Ash Wednesday" of T. S. Eliot answered:

> *Teach us to care and not to care*
> *Teach us to sit still*
> (New York: The Fountain Press, 1930)

66

The mind stilled is the mind at peace. There are few things in life more powerful than a peaceful mind.

The beloved mind leads to joy. Knowing that we have a "fourth response" is enough to fill the soul with joy. Participating with God in creating compelling and innovative solutions for new challenges brings joy. Dialoguing and dancing with other beloved minds in the ministry of restoration and renewal bring joy. On these fronts and others, joy is an uncontested, but all too often unacknowledged, energizer for creating and sustaining vibrant persons and organizations. Where there is joy, there is vital energy to be used in manifold, magnificent, and meaningful ways.

Living at a Sacred Pace: The Power of Noticing

Sacred pace is an alternative to living life in a hurry. It is doing so by making an intentional effort to see more clearly the ordinary and the extraordinary, listen more carefully to sounds and silences, and think more deeply, especially about those ideas and thoughts that stimulate new growth and positive change. I discuss each of these elements in my book *Addicted to Hurry: Spiritual Strategies for Slowing Down.* I will not repeat here what I've previously said. Suffice it for me to say here that in the seven years that have elapsed since my first writings on hurry addiction, the need to cultivate a sacred pace has never been more important. If anything, the hurry problem has gotten worse. And we continue to bless chronic speed with religious affirmation. I have a picture in my files of a young man walking alone with a shirt reading, "Jesus is coming back; look busy."

Perhaps the primary culprit regarding hurry's sustained hold on us is our easy acceptance of multitasking. We have gotten used to doing multiple things simultaneously, as fast as possible. It has become our way. Yet the price we pay in errors made, surface relationships, and muted creativity is, I believe, too high. Sometimes I imagine having a special day to cause us to wake up and envision a richer pace of living characterized by lavish amounts of awareness, patience, and peace. I suggest calling such a day One-Thing-at-a-Time-Day. This would be a day in which all persons would be encouraged to resist all multitasking and focus on doing one thing at a time, calmly, deliberately, and where possible, with great pleasure. That wouldn't be so bad, would it?

I have found no greater inspiration for living at a sacred pace than Jesus. His pace to me now is as important as his pronouncements. An example of Jesus living at a sacred pace and his not falling to all is found in Luke's Gospel, chapter 8, verses 40-42:

> When Jesus returned, the crowd welcomed him, for they were all waiting for him. Just then there came a man named Jairus, a leader of the synagogue. He fell at Jesus' feet and begged him to come to his house, for he had an only daughter, about twelve years old, who was dying.

"They were all waiting for him." You bet they were. Jesus was heading back to his home region after a rather noteworthy evangelistic crusade. Along with preaching captivating sermon-stories, Jesus had allegedly, through the power of his spoken word, halted a storm and cured a man possessed by demons. Is it any wonder that Jesus would have trouble sneaking back into town unnoticed?

Chances are, some in the crowd had needs of their own, none of which rivaled the great challenges that Jesus faced with the storm and the demons. Surely, Jesus would have a moment to hand out a few minor miracles. Maybe others in the welcoming party just came to watch, and perhaps shake his hand and say, "Way to go, Jesus!"

What I want you to note from the text is that though "all" waited for him for whatever reasons, Jesus responded to the request of just one, Jairus, whose daughter was deathly ill. Though confronted and surrounded with tens if not hundreds of legitimate concerns, demands, and expectations, Jesus gave himself permission to choose one matter for the moment.

Single-mindedness is an endangered practice. We are conditioned to do multiple things at a time. It has become our way of life, our oppressive obsession. What a liberating blessing of grace and space, to give ourselves permission to choose one over all, more often than not.

Jesus ministered at a sacred pace, allowing time for sufficient appreciation of life and rest for renewal. Consider the following testimonies of Jesus pacing Himself found in the Gospels:

"Jesus went out of the house and sat by the sea" (Matthew 13:1b, NKJV).

"He went out and departed to a solitary place" (Mark 1:35, NKJV).

"He departed and went into a desert place" (Luke 4:42, NKJV).

"Jesus being weary, sat on a well" (John 4:6, paraphrase).

The Blessing of Watching

Claude Monet's painting *Regatta at Sainte-Adresse* showcases a blue sky filled with clouds that look like extra-large fluffy pillows, a body of water that seems in places to bear foot-prints, nine visible small boats with equally tall sails already on the water, and a blue one, just coming from or about to enter the water, and most noteworthy for me, several smartly dressed people, seated or standing on a generously sanded beach, just watching it all.

I look at the picture, and I am drawn more not to what the people are looking at but to the people themselves. I wonder what they, these unnamed ones on beachside not to board boats but to behold them, are seeing. The picture reminds me of being on long drives on the bayou roads of Louisiana in my youth and observing persons who were, it seemed, just sitting on their porches, just looking at the cars go by or not.

The fictitious persons on the beach and the real ones on the porch have something important in common: they were not ashamed of watching for watching's sake. Time to watch for watching's sake allows us to behold beauty for beauty's sake, and life for life's sake, with no questions necessarily asked or answered. To just watch is to let living be living on its own terms for a moment, and seeing what will happen or not. Contentment and surprise are equally attended to or not.

In a life filled with schedules, e-mails, texts, and calls, the faint and thus easily missed call to just watch is one we need to heed more often. In watching, there are cleansing and catching, sensing and soaring, and most important of all, being for being's sake and being content and surprised by enchantments that are out of the reach of doing anything except watching.

Yield to Your Sacred Inner Flame

Mary Oliver is one of the world's premier poets and one of my very favorites. The case for her magnificence may be made

70

by referring to her magical way with ordinary words or her mighty way of seeing the magical splashed all over the ordinary world. Perhaps even more persuasive than both these praise arguments is something as simple as a child's choice. Once, when asked how she discovered poetry, Mary Oliver responded as follows:

> By myself. I would go into Cleveland to a used bookstore. They were very nice to me. I'd go down in the basement with a dust cloth and come up with these treasures. I'd go home with another load of books. The only record I broke in high school was for truancy. I'd put some books in a knapsack and go to the woods. And I got away with it. (Amy Sutherland, "Mary Oliver: Poet and Wanderer in the Woods," *Boston Globe*, November 3, 2012)

Can you see a young girl pouring over old books and dusting them off to get a better look at their titles? Can you see her making her way back home carrying her bag of books with both her hands? Can you see her making her way to one of her favorite spots in the woods and opening the first book of the day with eyes wide and soul smile even wider?

The feelings we have when we loose and lose ourselves in what we love, and what we perceive somehow loves us back, are Holy Fire. Such a feeling is a cauldron of creative energy and power extraordinarily beneficial not only to lovers, in this case a budding poet and her books, but also to the world at large. The grand gift of lavish personal love is social benevolence. This is the splendid and memorable wisdom of legendary sage Howard Thurman, who once advised someone seeking vocational guidance, "Don't ask what the world needs. Ask what makes you come alive, and go do it. Because what the world needs is people who have come alive" (Gil Bailie, *Violence Unveiled*, [New York: Crossroad, xv]). *Yielding to your sacred inner flame is your best offering to the world.*

Tending to the Space between Sleep and Wakefulness

Were you aware that you wake up on fertile ground each morning? The space between coming out of sleep and being fully awake is ripe. It is filled with dream messages that can enlighten. Additionally, one's own inner voice may be heard more clearly in a space not yet filled with the voices of others. Moreover, this is a time when the mind has not gone into hard think mode. It is still soft and open to matter we may too easily reject via our hard-nosed critical reflection. Finally, it is easier for us to hear God's voice when our own voice, as well as the voices of others, has not yet taken center stage.

Don't miss the blessings of early-morning soft-consciousness. Place a notebook, recorder, or other device near your bed so that you may be ready to receive the gifts of first-waking awareness. Your simply showing such readiness to receive will have you receiving more. We often have not because we expect not. Expect beautiful breakthroughs!

Walking Well in the Valley

It seems there is an unwritten requirement among certain Christians that persons need to feel upbeat all the time or something is wrong. I think there is something wrong with that expectation. Upbeatness is certainly a joyful experience; enthusiasm is a gift of life. But enthusiasm is not all of life. The fact is that no one goes through life without going through the valley. The valley may be an assortment of things, including but not limited to the following low places: disappointment, grief, pain, depression, worry, and failure. Or the valley may just be the result of having expended so much energy that you just don't have the energy or the will to feel up. That would be the valley of fatigue.

Whatever the cause or nature of life's low places, awareness helps us to live well there by owning them as legitimate locales in life, sacred places where we are not—and should not be made to feel—any less human or holy, but on the contrary, places where we, by seeing and noticing more softly than usual, may learn lessons about what it is to become more fully human and holy.

There were valleys in the life of Jesus, including the wilderness at the beginning of his ministry and the garden at the end of it, and there is no indication that he tried to avoid or rush through any of them. Nor should we. There are lessons in life such as patience, resilience, and deep peace apart from what may or may not be happening that cannot be learned on the mountaintop, no matter how high the mountain. Certain precious gems of life may be found only in the low places, places where, because God is everywhere, God is, as much as God is anywhere else.

P.S. The foregoing section was written after journaling about my feeling down one morning. As I owned where I was in the moment, before I realized it, I was typing this section of the book. Reflecting on this unscheduled writing moment says something about the power of the valley to surface strengths and understandings we never saw coming. Another name for that would be "grace."

Enhancing the Journey through Journaling

Journaling is a proved tool for cultivating living awareness in general and self-awareness in particular. In one of the best books on the beloved practice, *One to One: Self-Understanding through Journal Writing*, Christina Baldwin offers the following testimony:

> To keep a journal of self-awareness allows you to be an active leader in your own life, to learn from experience in ways that would be nearly impossible without the commitment to reflective and active writing. The journal creates a dialogue within yourself. It provides a forum for asking questions, suggesting alternatives, tracking the path of growth, and altering it as you go. ([New York: M. Evans and Company, 1977], 60)

And to think, when I started out journaling, it was just to record my experiences in my first pastorate. I had no idea that journaling would provide me with a ready way to not just remember, but reorder, reconnect, reroute, and re-create my life over and over again. Thus, there is no aspect of life for which journaling can't be made relevant and used as a support. Two of the most significant usages of journaling for me have been in the areas of negotiating trying terrains of transition and managing difficult turns in relationships. Being able to name and reflect on what was happening led to conjuring alternative perspectives and actions. In this mighty way, journaling may serve as a significant tool for life empowerment.

Journaling cultivates an attitude of responsibleness for one's own life and a creative disposition toward life. We can go for days without noticing the deeper meaning of our thoughts, feelings, and interactions. Life becomes a blur instead of the magnificent bounty that it is. When it is all too easy to taste just the top of our living, journaling is a way to go deeper into our lives and perhaps discover diamonds that may increase our overall sense of enchantment in the world. Moreover, journaling is a way to chronicle the deepest dialogues of the soul and chart the mysterious passageways of one's communion with

God. Christina Baldwin writes the following in her book *Life's Companion: Journal Writing as a Spiritual Practice*:

> The spiritual journey is the one trip we are all taking together. You may be in a bookstore, a grocery store, a restaurant, or home in bed. Whatever you think you're doing, whatever else you identify as happening, you are also somewhere in the middle of your spiritual journey. The spiritual journey is the part of life that is the path within the path. Spirituality is the sacred center out of which all life comes, including Mondays and Tuesdays and rainy Saturday afternoons in all their mundane and glorious detail. The spiritual journey is what the soul is up to while we attend to daily living. The spiritual journey is the soul's life comingling with ordinary life. The fabric tears: the soul sees Monday, Monday sees the soul. ([New York: Bantam, 1990], 3)

"What's Going On?" is the title of one of legendary singer Marvin Gaye's greatest hits. His melodic inquiry was directed toward becoming more attuned to turbulent society. While journaling takes into consideration the matters of the outer, it is as interested in what's going on within the inside. Therefore, our journals become holy grounds of discussions we can have in no other place. But because we can have them there, we can know, we can grow, and we can go on. Journaling helps us to journey on with greater wisdom, deeper peace, and no small joy.

75

CHAPTER SIX

{ AWARENESS OFFERINGS FOR LEADERSHIP }

Gratitude changes attitude.
A changed attitude alters perception.
An altered perception reveals new possibilities.
—KBJ

*A*wareness, as in greater sensitivity to life and greater appreciation for certain fabulously liberating truths about life, can enhance leadership in numerous ways. The following are benefits I've realized in my own ministry and suggest you may expect in yours.

Greater Sensitivity to Your Spiritual and Emotional Well-Being

Being conscious of the state we are in is a valuable tool for leadership. Poor decisions are more avoidable with an accurate assessment of a depleted mental state. To the end of understanding better when you are ready to go, and when you need to go take a break, here are some indicators I have found to be personally helpful.

Seven Signs That You Are Running on Empty

1. *You haven't had a day off in weeks.* Due to obligatory weekend labor in a society when most persons have the weekends off and a vocation that requires appropriate attention be paid to emergencies, pastors are particularly prone to working multiple weeks in succession without taking vital and necessary time off. This is a prescription for disaster.

2. *You feel like you're rushing all the time.* In a world where fast and faster are promoted and praised as our only options, it is easy to run and keep running simply because everyone else is doing so. Chronic rushing risks our being in attendance where life is concerned, but not present.

3. *You are beginning secretly to resent the obligations placed on you.* Smiles don't tell the whole story. Often, smiles hide deep-seated tensions and stress. We laugh to keep from crying. As pastors, in the course of trying to be all things to all people, all the time, we cultivate the tragic skill of being able to hide our pain from others and from ourselves.

4. *You are increasingly impatient.* Sadly, the first ones to feel the brunt of our lack of gracious waiting are our family members, especially our children. One of the signs of impatient waiting is rushed listening.

5. *You are becoming more forgetful.* When everything starts meshing together in a life characterized by overload and hurry, life loses its distinctiveness. We lose the ability to tell one thing from another and, at times, the ability to name one thing to recall and remember.

6. *You tend not to be excited about life.* Living excitement may be gauged, in part, by how much anticipation we feel for the day's plans and activities as we arise in the morning.

7. *You feel down and depressed more often than not.* What are being referred to here are not the occasional days and sometimes periods of feeling blue. Such a feeling periodically is a

part of wholesome living. Some of life's most important lessons can be learned only in the valley. On the other hand, taking up residence in despondency and despair is a sign of dangerously strained emotional and spiritual health.

The Power of Touch in Ministry

Since I came upon it some years ago, I have taped a small quotation by the esteemed Desmond Tutu to my church office desk: "Be gentle with God's people." Awareness cultivates a sense of gentle touch in ministry. By touch I mean accurate and appropriate sensibility and sensitivity in ministry. Here is a contemporary example of just the right touch in ministry applied at a tender time and place in ministry.

A fabulously compassionate, confident, and creative young pastor I know is having a promising beginning at a church. Tangible testimony of this is the church's moving forth with a significant building enhancement. They are doing so even as they expend emotional energy welcoming their new pastor, while continuing to grieve the sudden death of their beloved pastor of four decades. How has this young pastor, with bold, new, innovative ideas for ministry, some of which have already been introduced, been able to progress so far so fast? In part, it is due to something as simple and as necessary as touch.

His compassion for his congregants and his understanding of their hurt and esteem for their beloved deceased pastor are discernible in the way he talks and walks with his congregants. In fact, the building enhancement initiative is named for the beloved former pastor and will bear his portrait. The Sunday I was present, I marveled as the church displayed comparable enthusiasm for both their new memorial to their valiant former pastor and the fresh church and community initiatives being introduced by their visionary new pastor.

I believe the new pastor is being given the green light of leadership because he has given the green light of respect to his church's history and the revered place of his beloved predecessor. It is all too common for new pastors to be intimidated by and begin to compete with a beloved leader's continued presence in the minds and hearts of church members. In a contrasting and compelling light of an example, this new pastor, comfortable in his skin and the embrace of a loving family, is gently and genuinely joining the church in remembering well: *holding fond memories in a way that waves on rather than holds up a church's forward momentum and movement. Tradition is best served when it inspires progress.*

One of the crucial underrated skills for ministry is touch. Perhaps this is true because we need to understand more deeply how important compassion and empathy are for ministry. With much due attention given to updating strategies and technologies for ministry, it is easy to miss fully appropriating ministry's basic initial strength as shown by Jesus: genuinely caring about people. There is no real ministry apart from believing that people really matter. Fundamental to understanding the value of the personhood of others is appreciating yourself as a person. And perhaps this is the root of the challenge. There is less of an impulse to touch others in love if we are not in touch with ourselves as the Beloved of God. We touch as we have been touched. It has been said that wounded persons wound others. It is even more true that healed persons heal others, first and foremost, by their very being. Our ability to be with people and to tailor our communication with them sensitively and wisely based on a full appreciation for who they are as children of God is informed by our personal experience with God's love and grace.

Touch is as important as truth. Without the right touch, the truth we think we speak may be distorted and misunderstood. How often do we say and do the right things at the wrong times and in the wrong ways? Boldness and gentleness are not opposites. Truth with touch goes a long way.

Here are a few ways to cultivate touch in ministry as it relates to pastoral conversation, including counseling and administrative situations.

1. *Speak with persons, allowing ample space for listening to what they are saying.*

2. *Be open to receiving signals from others that may lead you to adjust things that you have planned to say.* As in preaching, communication is not stating what we planned to say exactly as we planned to say it. Communication is being open to the person and the moment and tailoring speech to the influences of the same.

3. *Review your dialogue with persons in your journaling, especially encounters that did not go well.* Rehearse what was said. Imagine what might have been said that may have created a more productive encounter.

In pastoring, there is no more important place for touch than the handling of heritage, particularly in churches with long histories fondly remembered. Many a young maverick pastor has fallen on the plains of planned reformation. The fall is often due to not providing sufficient proof of regarding as important, if not precious, that which was to be reformed. Respectful appreciation, delicately placed, is a powerful tool for meaningful and joyful progress.

Enhanced Listening

Edward Kennedy "Duke" Ellington, a man whom Andre Previn once called "one of the four great modern composers," wrote more than three thousand original works, recording more than three hundred times. A poster of Mr. Ellington adorns my home office door. Based on a picture by Girolamo

Ramelli, the shot captures Ellington in a contemplative pose, gazing into the far-off distance and, seemingly just as much, the distance deep within.

Episode 5 of Ken Burns's epic *Jazz* documentary begins with Ellington seated at a piano. After he plays a bit, an interviewer asks, "Where do you get your ideas from?" Ellington responds, "Ideas? Oh, man, I got a million dreams. That's all I do is dream. All the time." Next, Ellington plays some more and then strikingly confesses that his piano playing is really "dreaming" (Ken Burns, *Jazz,* episode 5, "Swing: Pure Pleasure," 2000, Florentine Films). This exchange comes to mind because central to Ellington's "dreaming" in the film is his listening. The segment begins with Ellington covering one of his ears. When he plays, or dreams, the left hand comes down, and he is all ears. His listening is visible, purposeful, and intense, so much so that you can almost hear him listening. Moreover, his listening is accented by the sparseness of musical notes. His playing has as much silence in it as it has sound. Though the silences are "rests" in musical terms, in reality Ellington is not resting in such spaces. He is hard at work listening, at one point even squinting his eyes, in delicate yet relentless search of a hidden note.

We have created a speeded-up, blurry world in which seeing and listening can be hard to do. Among our sacrifices is what Ellington seemed to have in abundance: creativity. Noted ones in various fields agree on the prominence of observing and listening, in a word, noticing.

Once during a business meeting, I was caught off guard by a member's cold demeanor. Several times during the session, she was noticeably curt and short with fellow members. She was also particularly antagonistic regarding a proposal I submitted, in a manner that I felt was unusually out of place. That being the case, I resisted challenging her. Throughout the meeting, I kept feeling in my spirit that something was wrong. Perhaps she did have understandable problems with the proposal, but something else was going on. My impression was that she was not really responding to the meeting matter at all but to something else. After the meeting, I went to her and asked if there was anything wrong. Her eyes began to fill with water as she told me about her garden that had been trampled over by uncaring youth just hours before. Her heart was broken. Any communication with any chance of ready passage would have to acknowledge her broken heart. As I reflect on that moment, I realize that my choice not to challenge her (and there are times when the pastor's choice should be different) was a way of sensing her pain, though I didn't know what it what it was I was sensing exactly. Touch may not be readily understood in the moment, but its usage must be forever at the ready for the pastor who would grow in congregational effectiveness and respect.

Pastoral touch involves listening in the spaces between the words. People go through so much from day to day. Our plans and proposals may be uppermost on our minds, but the pastor honed in tender touch knows that such plans and proposals have a better chance of being received as we learn how not to run roughshod over the feelings and wounds of persons. There is no way of knowing such feelings and wounds apart from deepening compassion and empathy, apart from listening.

Preaching from a Place of Love

I once asked the widow of a stellar preacher what she thought was the key to her husband's great preaching. Without hesitation, she offered, "My husband loved people." I once heard someone refer to legendary Grambling football coach

Eddie Robinson's philosophy of coaching. Coach Robinson felt that you had to love players in order to really coach them. I believe the best gospel preaching stems from love: love of people, love of message, love of God, and lest we forget, love of self.

Thus, I believe that the task of the preacher, not only for sermon preparation but also for life preparation, is to receive and keep on receiving God's supreme love. Too many, too often, preach love without feeling loved.

More than being impressed by our communicative prowess and theological intelligence, listeners will have from the supremely loved preacher a sense and feeling of God's supreme love, in our words, our silences, our body language, our spirit.

Preaching from a love supreme, to borrow the title of John Coltrane's musical masterpiece, opens the possibility for preaching preparation and performance that allows preacher-leaders to excavate and survey three hidden gems of preaching:

1. *Preaching with a lighter touch in which we use words more to discover and uncover than to defend or define.* Due to our having worked on a sermon for some time, and our wanting people to receive well the one public standard by which we are seen and evaluated weekly, preaching can come across as being excessively heavy. This heaviness may be added to by a philosophy of preaching that holds as its goal convincing and persuading people. Congregants may add even more to the heaviness of preaching with their expectation of simple and easy solutions. To preach with a lighter touch is to, while working arduously at sermon preparation, be relieved of the burden of having to convince anyone of anything. To preach with a lighter loving touch is to preach with a goal of inspiring curiosity and

imagination, that listeners may be compelled further to engage a continuing conversation with the Lover of their souls.

2. *Preaching from a place of contentment where we don't preach for acceptance but from acceptance.* Each sermon opportunity offers a choice of persons accepting or not accepting the things we say. If we are not careful, acceptance by listeners can become the primary target of preaching. When this happens, the preaching message and voice is severely compromised. While the perceived response of the listener on the part of the preacher is one important tool for effective sermonizing, it is not the regulating one. The preacher for whom acceptance or rejection by persons is no longer the main focus is free to preach with greater abandon, freedom, and pastoral-prophetic relevancy, offering what persons may or may not *want* to hear, but *need* to.

3. *Preaching with what David Whyte calls "investigative vulnerability," preaching that doesn't pretend through content and tone to know more than it knows.* It is preaching that seeks to have a continuing friendship with mystery, and more than anything else invites its listeners to do the same. Feeling supremely loved offers a deeply rooted emotional, mental, and spiritual confidence. The positive fall-out from this is not having to overly contrive and construct pastoral authority from anything that we know or say. We can risk being vulnerable in our teaching and preaching, knowing that our ultimate sense of value is beyond any word or deed, our own or anyone else's. Such a graced disposition more naturally and easily manifests itself in preaching tones that avoid dogmatic, rock-solid sureties. Rooted in unearned unconditional holy affirmation, we are led to be more relaxed and open in our preaching, daring to preach and teach with all doors and windows flung open wide for the fresh winds of the Spirit blowing from within and

without. Such preaching is acknowledging of our limited view of truth, welcoming of questions, and encouraging of persons to see a sermon as but an imperfect part of our continuing personal and communal, humbling, amazing, and ever-revealing dialogue with God.

Sense Rinse

There are few things in life

more deeply,

mysteriously,

and soulfully

satisfying

than

simply

easing back

and

listening

to the rain.

—KBJ

Question at 3 AM

Will you

claim the

elegant expanse

of your

Holy Spirit?

—KBJ

Wow; Wow!

We look outside

at a beautiful day

and say, "Wow!"

The angels look inside

at our beautiful souls

and say, "Wow!"

—KBJ

Wait and See

Sometimes

the best prayer of all

is to just sit in the sunlight,

and remember,

should it be temporarily

blocked from your view

that light hidden for a moment

is no less light,

just wait

and see.

—KBJ

{ THE SPIRITUALITY OF PLAY }

Without play, without that child still alive in all of us,
we will always be incomplete. And not only physically,
but creatively, intellectually, and spiritually as well.
—George Sheehan

And who else could this be, who goes off . . .
carrying his sandals, and singing?
—Mary Oliver, referring to Jesus

When we lose the ability or willingness to be vulnerable,
joy becomes something we approach with deep foreboding.
—Brené Brown

The Spiritual Power of Play

I never saw it coming. I never thought I would be writing about play as an essential element of spirituality. The first time play came was as a pastor one day as I was officiating at a funeral. Unfortunately, the service was scheduled for noon, recess time at the elementary school next door. A summer day in an air-condition-less church meant that a large side door was open facing the children rushing out to play. Great. Just before I stood to conduct a solemn ceremony of departure, children were running, jumping, and laughing. They were having fun, and there I was trying to have a funeral.

I began feeling aggravated about the obvious conflict and contradiction: deep grief would now have to compete with delight, of all things. It was then that I heard from upper management, and I am not talking about the church's board of trustees. I am referring to God. I heard a question being asked of me that I certainly had not the time or interest in formulating: *What do you think the deceased is doing now in my Presence?* I sat silent, stunned, and speechless. Graciously, I soon learned that the question was rhetorical: she is running, jumping, and laughing, so glad to be home. From that moment on, play was something to me that it had never been before: spiritual prayer and play are siblings.

Prodded to a deeper study, I discovered that early play theorists, most notably Johan Huizinga and D. W. Winnicott, linked play to personal growth and cultural advancement decades ago. In his classic *Homo Ludens,* Huizinga writes, "Pure play is one of the main bases of civilization." Winnicott observes, "In playing, and perhaps only in playing, the child or adult is free to be creative" (*Playing & Reality* [New York: Tavistock Publications, 1971], 53).

Through the years, many other provocative declarations and suggestions have been made concerning the powers of play, none more singularly comprehensive and potent than the following witness rendered by Stephen Nachmanovitch in his priceless volume *Free Play: Improvisation in Life and Art:*

> To play is to free ourselves from arbitrary restrictions and expand our field of action. Our play fosters richness of

response and adaptive flexibility. This is the evolutionary value of play—play makes us flexible. By reinterpreting reality and begetting novelty, we keep from becoming rigid. Play enables us to rearrange our capacities and our very identity so that they can be used in unforeseen ways. ([New York: Jeremy P. Tarcher, 1990], 43)

Books such as *Play* by Stuart Brown and *The Power of Play* by David Elkind have appeared along with lead stories in respected business and science journals heralding the need to inject more playfulness in our personal and vocational lives. Such discussions are of no small importance at a time when many organizations, including many churches, are struggling to survive amid institutional decay, dysfunction, and dormancy, and are sorely in need of new, creative wellsprings and the faithful confidence to be nourished by them.

As play kept on coming, I began coming across readings that explained more specifically how it was and is that play is a deeply spiritual engagement. For wonder of a writer and spirit-person Madeleine L'Engle, the enchanting diamond of playfulness is what she calls unself-consciousness:

When we are *self*-conscious, we cannot be wholly aware; we must throw ourselves out first. This throwing ourselves away *is* the act of creativity. So, when we wholly concentrate, like a child in play, or an artist at work, then we . . . escape our self-conscious selves. . . .

When we can play with the unself-conscious concentration of a child, this is: art: prayer: love. (*Glimpses of Grace* [San Francisco: HarperSanFrancisco, 1996], 162–63)

Just like that, Jesus' tease to Nicodemus one night that he must be "born again" sounds more like the God-delightful truth.

No, I never saw play coming. But when I put all of this together with what Jesus said one day about adults becoming as children in order to enter the Kingdom, maybe I should have; maybe we all should have. *In God's way of lavish grace, why wouldn't something so essential be so natural?*

As I daydream about it now, my whole revelatory experience about playfulness is akin to hearing a big balloon go POP! Then, I turn and see countless larger balloons of various colors appear. Somehow I sense and satisfy the impulse to grab hold of as many of them as I can, and I go sailing higher and higher into the fearless distance, laughing as I go.

P.S. John Ayto offers the following in his *Dictionary of Word Origins*:

> The origins of play are obscure. It had a relative in Middle Dutch *pleien* "dance about, jump for joy," but this has now died out, leaving it in splendid but puzzling isolation, its ancestry unaccounted for. ([New York: Arcade Publishing, 1990], 398)

Did you get that? As is God, play is a mystery!

The God Who Calls Us to Play

Making a place for play in our vision of spirituality necessarily means that understandings of God and ministry will be challenged and transformed. As we undergo such changes, we may be surprised to see the wealth of witnesses who have viewed such esteemed matters in extremely lighthearted ways. Take for instance the following godly and playful prayer and poem.

In his golden book of prayers, *The Heart of God*, Rabindranath Tagore places before us the possibility that God is One who plays and invites us to enter into divine play:

Play Time

When my play was with You, I never questioned who You were. I knew no shyness or fear; my life was boisterous.
([Boston: Turtle Publishing, 1997], 66)

My friend, Desne Crossley, has written a magnificent poem published in *Becoming Fire* (Andover Newton Press, 2006) entitled "Gone Creativity." Her lament is a new welcome to her girl that has up and left her,

who makes art
with her way-out ideas and magic.

Such is the spirit of our common lament and welcome as we renew our love of holy play.

Play: Sacred Absorbing Pleasure

"Play" and its essential elements of absorption and pleasure are our sure way to joy. To be fully absorbed is to be so taken up with something that we lose all sense of time. Pleasure is our experience of being thoroughly delighted. What if God's will for each of us is to have as many experiences of sacred absorbing pleasure as possible, to play in the spirit?

Now if that sounds too selfish and hedonistic, step back with me for a moment, especially if you are a parent, guardian, or grandparent, and ask yourself this question: What brings you the most joy when observing your youthful loved ones? Not a few of you are ready with an answer immediately: seeing them happy. Why do you suppose it would be any different with God, our heavenly parent? What if, more than anything, God is delighted by our delight? What if, most of all in life, God wants to see us having the time of our lives? Suddenly, Jesus' words, "Except you become as a little child, you cannot enter

into the Kingdom," take on a strikingly powerful new meaning. Maybe Jesus was asking us to consider the playful spirit of
children as the key to kingdom living, now and later. Children
don't ask for permission to play; they just do. Children don't
seek to justify their play; they just do. It is as if they innately
know what their purpose is in the world and why they are here.
Come to think of it, about more than a few things, children
just know, and before it is "adult-ed," they more easily trust
their knowing.

The unsuspecting but unusually close relationship between
playfulness, especially as celebrated by children, and spirituality arises for me as well when I think of something Thomas
Merton wrote. In a moment of scintillating inspiration, Merton
reflected, "Some things are too clear to be understood." In just
eight words, Merton beholds and honors the accessibility and
inaccessibility of those things that are most worth knowing.
Perhaps, those best capable of playing with such a maddening and enlivening paradox—paradoxes do tend to be the best
truths of all—are the children and the most childlike among
us.

Speaking of Merton, what he wrote concerning play and
labor is, I believe, well worth your attention as you plant what
may be new seeds of contemplation regarding their kinship:

> Do not push too hard with the work, God will take care
> of everything, and will give you strength to do all that
> needs to be done. . . . In these days you should be car-
> ried by Him toward your destination, and do what you
> do more as play than as work, which does not mean that
> it is not serious: for the most serious thing in the life of a
> Christian is play. The seriousness of Christian play is the
> only genuine seriousness. Our work, when it develops the
> seriousness of worldly accomplishment, is sad indeed, and
> it does nothing. . . . All life is in reality the playing and

dancing of the Child-God in His world, and we, alas, have not seen it and known it. (*Echoing Silence: Thomas Merton on the Vocation of Writing,* ed. Robert Inchausti [Boston: New Seeds Books, 2007], 198–99)

As you end this brief chapter on the spirituality of play, I would like to ask you to consider the following questions that may prepare you for considering a subject you may never have thought of in theological and spiritual ways until now:

What was your favorite toy as a youth?

How did you feel when you were a child at play?

Is there a similarity between the feelings you had/have during play and the feelings you have during worship?

Where do you see God and Jesus at play in scripture?

How do you envision our play being pleasing to God?

Could it be that our play has the potential to create in and with God that which God chooses not to playfully create by God's Self?

What more can you say or ask about the creative power of play?

CHAPTER EIGHT

{ CULTIVATING A PLAYFUL DISPOSITION }

There must be energized imagination. In my mind, I must play with all manner of creative possibilities in my relations with others, familiarizing myself with the flavor of people and their potentiality.
—*Howard Thurman*

Howard Thurman: The Playful Prophet of the Soul

In my early thirties, I experienced ministry burnout. Two sentences helped to change my life. The first was a physician's simple but pointed and penetrating question: What do you do to relax? The second was a writer's prayer: [God,] "teach us how to respond to the needs of Thy children in ways that do not undermine the self, but inspire and enliven the spirit." The writer's name is Howard Thurman. Beloved by thousands the world over, Howard Thurman's writings have a way of gently but mightily touching and lifting heart and soul. His book *The Centering Moment* served as potent healing balm for me during my time of recovery from having overdosed on overcommitment. So healed by his words, I kept reading him, and I kept being renewed. When the opportunity came to teach about him at Andover Newton Theological School, I jumped at it. Teaching a course I named after his magnificent autobiography, *With Head and Heart*, has been one of the grandest thrills of my life.

As meaningful to me as anything else about my learning and sharing regarding Howard Thurman is discovering the playful dimensions of his spirituality. This sacred sage known for his depth of perception and thought also doodled, painted, and, get this, loved penguins. Listen to the confessions of the playful prophet offered in *With Head and Heart*:

> I have had a secret desire to paint pictures ever since I was a child. I like to doodle while my thoughts are otherwise engaged, to see where my unconscious mind will go.

He credits Peggy Strong, "one of the most resourceful human beings I have ever known," with helping his painting desire to blossom and flourish:

> It was she who urged me to paint. Once a week she would pick me up in San Francisco and drive me back to her cottage studio in Menlo Park. Our understanding was that she would not try to teach me to paint. She prepared the canvas, gave me paints and brushes, and left the rest to me. There is a heady quality of power and omniscience one feels making the stroke of brush translate in color a time-space vision available to anyone with eyes to see. The infinite range of shadings of color was a revelation. To look at a forest of green trees and see numberless variations of a single hue opened a new world of meaning to me.

Thurman turned himself loose in his delight and soon discovered a favorite painting subject: penguins:

My greatest joy has come from painting penguins. The initial inspiration came upon me during a visit to Vancouver. A penguin was hatched in the city zoo amid great excitement. On my way back east, I began sketching penguins. These developed into a series of oils, appropriately named "A Penguin on His First Date," "Two Drunk Penguins," "Penguin Politicians," and so on. Several of my friends sent me illustrated books about penguins, hoping, I suspect, that some similarity might develop between my paintings and the real thing. But to no avail. I paint the Penguin's View of Himself! When my friends say, "That doesn't look like a penguin to me," my answer is "Maybe not. But it does to the penguin." ([New York: Harcourt Brace Jovanovich, 1979], 240)

I find such confessions by Thurman to be not only delightfully enchanting but deeply profound and unusually helpful.

I am made to wonder about the significance and value of Thurman's play for his fruitful witness as a pastor, preacher, teacher, and author. When he speaks of "the infinite range of shadings of color," I observe Thurman being thrilled by art's blessing him with the further releasing of his own already eclectic and spacious spirit regarding religious and theological thought and practice.

When I hear Thurman playfully titling his penguin sketches, I marvel that his sketching and painting could infuse his capacity for freedom of imagination and expression, and thank God that such resources were at the ready for his richly varied and textured ministry.

When I hear him owning his unique representation of penguins, and wrapping that ownership in an imagined identification with penguins that others may not be privy to, my soul bends over backward in wild affirmation. What an amazing alternative to adopting a position of shame and ultra-defensiveness in the face of critique by others!

When I sense in Thurman a genuine bond with the beloved species of God we have come to call "penguins," I cherish the thought that just maybe unsung and unsuspected penguins (Thurman's experience with penguins predated the popular penguin movies and documentaries of recent years, including *Happy Feet, March of the Penguins,* and *The Penguins of Madagascar*) were a source of courage and inspiration for one who, as a dark-skinned African American male, though increasingly acclaimed, was not ever completely immune to the wounds inflicted by the sharp sword of racism. In this way, amid unseen heaviness of heart, play enabled Thurman to be "strangely light of heart," which novelist and writer Frederick Buechner suggests is the truest mark of a genuine saint.

In the end, I see play making Thurman more supple for holy transformation. The ripple effect continues to this day. Through allowing play to lift his holy human spirit, Howard Thurman was inspired and empowered to lift countless other holy human spirits. Such a spirit has no other choice but to play on.

The benefits of playfulness may not be immediately noticeable, but they are undeniable. Here are five ways I see playfulness abetting ministry:

1. *Freshness.* When one does so many of the same things over and over again, I don't care what those things are, boredom can set in. Ministry is not immune to this. The only way to remain fresh for the long haul is to be intentional about learning new things in familiar tasks. An experimental disposition is at the heart of playfulness. Playfulness primes us to be alert and creative, ever open to novelty and new growth.

2. *Dexterity.* Playfulness resists rigidness. In a spirit of play, we are more open to the Spirit's play of reforming and transforming—making all things new.

3. *Resilience.* No one is immune to a broken spirit and a broken heart. Yet, as we become more accustomed to living energized and inspired, we are less likely to have regular extended periods of feeling down.

4. *Boldness.* Fear keeps us aiming low in ministry or not aiming at all. The unsung antidote for fear is curiosity. Become interested in that which you fear, and suddenly, fear is melted away. Playfulness is a way to cultivate and satisfy curiosity.

5. *Contagiousness.* To be playful is to be lighthearted. Light is warming and attractive. As we let our lights shine bright in the spirit of ministry as holy play—exploration, creation, and celebration—chances are, we will spend less time searching for members and more time wondering where all of these people came from.

What other ways do you perceive playfulness blessing ministry?

Be Enchanted by Life on Purpose

What the flight attendant said to us all before we deplaned on April 29, 2007, on a flight from Columbia, South Carolina, to Washington, DC, was so surprisingly stimulating, I wrote it down as soon as my hands were free: "I hope you have a fabulous week, not only productive but enjoyable." It was as if she had cast a spell on us all. What an utterly unpredictable enchantment. I have since learned to expect to be enchanted, deeply moved in my heart and soul, by anyone, anyplace, and anytime. Moreover, I have learned that there are some things I can do to make enchantment more welcome in my life:

103

1. *Expect wonder and notice it when it arrives.* Legendary comedian Flip Wilson used to portray a flamboyant female personality whose favorite line was "What you see is what you get." In many ways, this funny line is a profound truth and one of the most important of all. What we see is as much in our minds as it is in front of our eyes. Perception and expectation are the ways we envision the world and imagine new worlds. That being said, if you wish to be marveled by life, begin with the expectation that you will be. This creates the attitudinal disposition, not to mention the energy, that makes it more likely to happen and makes you more keenly aware and appreciative of it when it does happen. There's a whole lot of marvel going on that we just miss because we don't expect to see it, and we spend little time honoring it when it appears.

2. *Behold blessings.* One evening, during the time of my writing this book, I had a strangely meaningful experience. I'd awakened, gone to the bathroom, and returned to bed. As I lay there, I found that my sinuses were blocked, so I started breathing through my mouth. Before long, I found myself being mindfully grateful for being able to have an additional mode of breathing. I was not limited to breathing through my nose. Then, I felt obliged to take deeper breaths, at which I felt, it seemed, spaces in my lungs feeling fresh breath they hadn't felt in a long while. Like many of you, no doubt, I reserve deep breathing for when I am asked to do so in a physician's office. I don't breathe as deeply as I should. At least, I didn't until that night. I began savoring more the filling and filling of my lungs with fresh evening air. I was breathing deeply and on purpose, and enjoying it, I soon noticed, not through my mouth but through my nose, the healthier way to breathe. In the celebration of breathing, my sinuses had cleared.

The word *behold* is usually reserved for use at the end of the year, when we remember the Christmas narrative in which extraordinary angels come through, asking anyone who will listen, it seems, to "behold." Beholding, holding and caressing with one's sight and soul, is too good to limit to just a few days a year. We become that which we focus on, that which we behold. Why not behold many blessings we are receiving all the time, including the blessing of breathing?

3. *Live with a grateful heart.* Beginning the day with gratitude is in order. When each of us comes to consciousness each day, we are in fact experiencing something of a wild surprise: life. Life! It is something that we did not earn, to our knowledge didn't do anything to deserve, and never saw coming. Being grateful for life at the start of the day sets the inner thermostat on thanks. There are far worse ways to stride through the day than to stride in thanks. Gratitude is a choice, one we can not only make, but make with an attitude. I remember passing a woman entering a church for a funeral one day and politely offering the greeting, "Good morning, how are you?" Her response has echoed in me since the moment I heard it: "I am too blessed to complain."

The Playground of Reading

Like perhaps many of you reading this book, I have been in love with reading. As a child, I would remain up late at night reading books about young athletes playing football. Soon, it was matters of religion. For some reason, Fulton J. Sheen's *The Life of Christ* had a special appeal to me. During the summers, I passed most of the time by reading through encyclopedias our parents purchased for us and books checked out of the library we could walk to. (What marvelous blessings for a child to have, parents who are visionary enough to invest in encyclopedias and a library accessible by foot.)

My reading adventure turned in a new direction when I saw a picture of a man on television one night. The news being reported had to do with his having been killed. But amazingly, on the night of his death, Martin Luther King Jr. became alive for me. I began reading books about him, and this thing called a civil rights movement. I loved reading. I loved getting lost in a story. I loved gaining new knowledge. I loved words, how they sounded, how they sounded together. I loved thinking about new questions that some books would place in my mind.

My reading grew more and more to focus on matters of my professions: ministry and teaching. By the time I was in my mid-twenties, out of seminary and into my first pastorate, I'd built up a pretty sizable library of books, and then something disturbing happened: I stopped reading; I stopped making time for it, which is an effective way to stop loving anything. Oh, I'd read a book here or there, and I'd study for sermon and Bible study preparation, but my thirst and passion for reading had been pushed away. I busied and overbusied my life with doing ministry.

A bout with burnout and a recommendation from a wise physician that I find things to do in order to relax initiated my return to reading for the love and joy of it. As I ponder reading's renewed importance in my life, I remember something Stephen King offers about writing in his valuable book *On Writing*: "When I'm writing, it's all the playground, and the worst three hours I ever spent there were still pretty damned good" ([New York: Scribner, 2000], 153). I can say the same thing not just about writing now, but about reading. If I am able to play on the ground of writing, it is because I played and play again first on the ground of reading.

Why am I telling you all of this? I want to encourage you to continue or renew or begin your reading life. Give lavish time and energy to it; unashamedly feel delight full and free for it. The enriched life is the savoring life. I believe we are blessed immeasurably as we dare to lose and loose ourselves in the things that we love. Reading is one such thing for me. It is so even more so these days as I consider reading to be handling radiant maps containing passageways and secrets of how the Great Adventurer God has inspired adventures of exploration and discovery in the lives of others. Mind you, I don't need "God" to be cast all over a book to be held spellbound by it. God does not have to be named to be known. God need not be acknowledged to be present. To this end, I believe all reading adventures to be potentially worth my while.

This is the point for me now, that when I am reading I am not just being informed and pleasured; I am being made privy to sides and dimensions of God that others have experienced via multifarious adventures, experiences, ideas, and theories. Reading grants us ready and easy (even more so these days with the arrival of smartphones and e-book readers) access to the wild wonder of it all. Reading is nothing to stop, dismiss, or do sparingly, or do just to get up a sermon. Reading is a way to play, to enter the play of God through others, dead and alive, in our world and beyond it. Can you detect how reading and interpreting reading in this way fill me and keep me full?

Yielding to Joyful Play

In a very deep sense I would say that the addiction, the drug addiction from which so many people suffer, is due to the fact that man cannot live a shallow life, stale. He needs exultation. He needs moments of celebration. One of the most important things is to teach man how to celebrate.
—Abraham Joshua Heschel

I am most comfortable now with seeing my purpose in life as yielding to whatever is calling me in a spirit of and to joyful play. And if I may say to you, if there is no sense of joy or play in what you do, chances are, you are not living in the area, the sacred playground, of your purpose.

One of my places of joyful play is doing exactly what I'm doing now, thinking and writing, and I am deeply moved by the words of writers who discuss their craft in playful terms. For example, Brenda Ueland offers the following advice in her gem of a classic, *If You Want to Write*:

> I learned that you should feel when writing, not like Lord Byron on a mountain top, but like a child stringing beads in kindergarten—happy, absorbed, and quietly putting one bead after another. ([St. Paul, MN: Graywolf Press, 1987], 50)

Joyful work is an act of devotion. Remember, the sweetest surrender of all is to give yourself over to that which is deeply and spiritually calling you. Do not be afraid to give lavish time, energy, attention, and passion to what you love. Therein is Holy Fire.

When We All Play Together

If at all possible, please listen to a selection before proceeding: "Diminuendo and Crescendo in Blue" on the album *Ellington at Newport*. If you cannot listen to the selection at this moment, you must promise yourself that you will and keep your promise. The selection is regarded by many as one of the most ecstatic moments in the history of jazz.

Each time I listen to this performance, I am grateful for the willingness of all to be free and, as people used to say in the church I grew up in, Mount Hermon Baptist Church, New Orleans, Louisiana, "let the Spirit have Its way."

Paul Gonsalves plays twenty-seven choruses on his horn caught ablaze, each one a new flame lit by a fresh match. Elaine Anderson dances as if she is dancing for the very first time or the last. A band that has ascended many musical mountains before discovers a magic mountain that is holy ground because it is momentarily limitless-sounding dancing ground, the likes of which they've never traveled before. An audience never second-guesses or hesitates but leaps into full free fall emotional expression, not caring where it will lead them or how it will leave them. And Duke Ellington has the devoted and deep Spirit sense simply to let it all happen, somehow feeling that this is the moment he has been headed toward for all of his life. Indeed, Ellington later said, "I was born at Newport." Jesus and a Pharisee named Nicodemus would understand.

Good news on good news, that moment long ago and all those who played together do not hold a monopoly on the elements in play that evening: *Risk, Abandon, Trust, Freedom, Joy.* Cultivating playfulness personally and congregationally releases those same powers in lavish abundance. It need not be a one-night affair. Oh, what faithful fun there is to be had, when we all play together, and expect to.

Leaders experience such moments in ministry when strikingly spirited events happen outside of our planning. For example, I remember during a worship service being asked at the eleventh hour if a group of students from a nearby university who had started attending our church could offer a musical selection, just before my sermon. I thought this was odd. I had not heard of any rehearsing having gone on and was not accustomed to making such decisions in the middle of worship. Yet, I allowed them to make their offering. What happened next was Pure Glory. Those young persons sang with such passion and beauty that it took the entire church by Holy Storm. In an instant, worship was transformed, and suddenly we all found ourselves on the mountaintop. My sermon ended up being an extended altar call. This was many years ago, yet I can still feel the power of that moment. In some ways, those college students have never stopped singing in my soul for good.

My point is that as we are open to the many varied ways God can move by God's Spirit in ways planned and unplanned, the very expectation is a great ministry energizer and sustainer.

By the way, for more on the wonder of what happened when the Spirit fell at Newport, Rhode Island, one night, read *Backstory in Blue: Ellington at Newport '56* by John Fass Morton (New Brunswick: Rutgers University Press). The testimonies, observations, and pictures will inspire you.

Laugh More

God will fill your mouth with laughter and your lips with shouts of joy.
—Job 8:21 (paraphrase)

Joy is the infallible sign of the presence of God.
—Madeleine L'Engle

Laughter is carbonated holiness.
—Anne Lamott

Deborah Blanchard, a writing-pastor and friend in ministry, offers the following reflection in a manuscript entitled "The Christmas Church":

> Laughter is a signpost of the presence of God which takes us over the threshold from who we were towards who we hope to become. Laughter opens up our heart, loosens the fears that wind us up, and prepares a place for the wisdom of God to take hold.

Healing and healthy laughter—that rises up from a common center of understanding, experience, and identification—is a gift from God. Laughter in worship reminds us not to take ourselves so seriously. Healthy moments of laughter in worship create an atmosphere of humility and awe, which prepares our hearts, minds, and souls for the nudging and teaching of God's Spirit. Worship—filled with a sense of gratitude, possibility and compassion for neighbors both near and far—creates an atmosphere of hope for those who have come. It is good to have a strong current of hope flowing through a service of worship. Hope is a treasure to take home with you—after you have made the effort to come.

Laughter is a signpost of God's presence, and it has been said that "humor is a prelude to faith and laughter is the beginning of prayer." People are so often filled with pain, fear, and sorrow that laughter alone will not bring healing. Seeds of faith cannot take root or grow unless the soil is deep enough to hold the laughter. Depth comes from an authentic sense of humility and awe, which is ready to pray, to learn, to share, and to serve. Embedding laughter within worship clearly signals the joy and the pain of life!

CHAPTER NINE

PLAY POWERS

{ }

Keep some room in your heart for the unimaginable.
—Mary Oliver

The Power of Jazz for Empowering Life and Ministry

When it comes to play, one of the great examples of it in my life is the playing of jazz. It is a musical power that prioritizes listening in the moment to other musicians, to the audience, and to the creative voice within that wants to make in the moment a musical contribution that's never been heard quite that way before. The spirit of improvisation at the heart of jazz is the spirit of being continually open to the Spirit and, along with others, discovering new musical ground. Martin Luther King Jr., once said of the monumental exemplary play known as jazz,

> Much of the power of our Freedom Movement in the United States has come from this music. It has strengthened us with its sweet rhythms when courage began to fail. (Dr. Martin Luther King Jr., "On the Importance of Jazz," Opening Address to the 1964 Berlin Jazz Festival)

Jazz continues to be mined for persons in many different fields. Seth Godin is one of the leading business thinkers and consultants in the world. His blog at www.SethGodin.com is read by thousands each day. It is the one blog I make sure to read each day because Godin does not waste words in presenting provocative insights. His blog post of November 13, 2012, "Effortless," was especially meaningful for me, as Godin comments on the fact that the listener can hear a few notes crack in the track *Harmonique.*

> Of course, Coltrane was completely capable of playing these notes correctly. And yet he didn't. . . .
>
> It's this effort and humanity that touches us about his solo, not just the melody. . . .
>
> Sometimes, "never let them see you sweat," is truly bad advice. The work of an individual who cares often exposes the grit and determination and effort that it takes to be present. . . .
>
> Perfecting your talk, refining your essay and polishing your service until all elements of you disappear might be obvious tactics, but they remove the thing we were looking for: you.

As a preacher and teacher, I immediately resonated with Godin's astute observation. Indeed, *effectiveness* and *perfection* are not synonyms. Authenticity, warts and all, is one of the most powerful forces a presenter has, if not the most powerful. Just as important as Godin's observation was Godin's example, John Coltrane. At this point, I encourage you to stop reading and download the selection mentioned by Godin, if you don't have it already. Listen, even if you don't particularly care for jazz; just listen once and better yet twice.

I was not surprised by Godin's choice of jazz icon John Coltrane. Jazz, for more than a decade now, has been one of the most important influences on my life and ministry, preaching in particular. If you are interested, you may learn more about how jazz can enhance your preaching by reading my book *The Jazz of Preaching: How to Preach with Great Freedom and Joy* or reviewing my seminary course syllabus at http://www.ants. edu/pdf/sp12_cmpr730s.pdf.

For now, I wish to identify a few ways I believe listening to jazz and learning more about it can enhance ministerial life and leadership.

Jazz Helps Us to Be Free and to Free Others

First, the spirit of jazz is the spirit of freedom. Before it is an art form, jazz is a bold expression of life amid the threats of deathliness and death itself. In his marvel of a book, *Treat It Gentle*, iconic New Orleans–born clarinetist Sidney Bechet goes one magnificent step further than the usual locating of the roots of jazz in the Sunday free day singing and dancing gathering of slaves in his enchanting city's Congo Square; he situates the birth of jazz with the unusually free frolicking spirit of his grandfather Omar:

> My grandfather—that's about the furthest I can remember back. My grandfather was a slave. But he was a man that could do anything. He could sing; he danced, he was a leader. It was natural to him; and everyone followed him. . . .
>
> Sundays when the slaves would meet—that was their free day—he beat out rhythms on drums at the Square— Congo Square they called it—and they'd all be gathered there around him. Everyone loved him. They waited for him to start things: dances, shouts, moods even. Anything he wanted to do, he'd lead them. He had a power. . . . [H]e was a free slave long before Emancipation. And he had his music and he could play it whenever he wanted.

115

Omar's unique gift was in owning always what most slaves only felt released inside of them on Sunday:

> But Sunday mornings it was different. He'd wake up and start to be a slave and then maybe someone would tell him: "Hell, no. Today's Sunday . . . free day." And then he'd hear drums from the square. First one drum, then another one answering it. Then a lot of drums. Then a voice, one voice. And then a refrain, a lot of voices joining and coming into each other. And all of it having to be heard. The music being born right inside itself, not knowing how it was getting to be music, one thing being responsible for another. Improvisation . . . that's what it was. It was primitive and it was crude, but down at the bottom of it—inside it, where it starts and gets into itself—down there it had the same thing there is at the bottom of ragtime. It was already born and making in the music they played in Congo Square. ([Boston: De Capo Press, 2002], 8)

Bechet's wondrous account focuses on the heart of jazz, a shout of freedom, not as something in the distance to be sought for, but as something within that was already alive and moving inside slaves' souls.

Such freedom is an essential reality for leadership. Only when leaders are free are they able to tap into their full powers. Only as they are free are they able to own their gifts without fear of reprisal. Moreover, free spirits impart freedom to all around them. The greatest gift you can give others is to support their being whom they really are, to help them to celebrate their own selves as free and full children of God.

As ministry leaders, perhaps it would encourage our souls and the souls of others to spend more time reflecting on how particular persons are growing as persons and in their roles as church leaders.

We spend so much time planning and critiquing ministry. Isn't celebrating the offerings of church members just as important? This can be done in small, simple ways, for example, a personal card, a conversation, or a public acknowledgment during worship. It may also be done at a special program where persons are asked to share specific ways they have been blessed by others in the church. My point is we can be far more intentional and creative when it comes to noticing and celebrating each other. In doing so, we will create a new well of positive spiritual energy for the church, empowering us all for more inspired being and doing in the world.

Jazz Is Co-Creative

Second, jazz provides leaders with a rich model for blending learning, preparation, and actual situation. The undoing of much of ministry is imposition: trying to impose whatever it is we know, or think we know, and just know the congregation should know, on people and the settings they have occupied and tended to long before our arrival. Often we are dismayed when persons don't get it. The problem, in part, is in the perception that ministry is something pre-set and packaged that we are divinely ordained to give people, whether they want it or not.

In jazz, personal feelings, fellow musicians, audience, setting, and the moment are just as important as learning and preparation. The goal is not to present something to persons that has been fabricated and produced beforehand but to join with persons in celebrating something that never has been experienced before. The goal is not imposition but co-creation. Only co-creation is significant enough to create greater humility within a leader and greater esteem that a leader holds for persons. Such attitudes are unsung but indispensable leadership traits of the highest order.

117

The mixing of prior learning and preparation with the matter of the moment is commonly referred to as *improvisation.* Improvisation, improperly understood, is making up something from nothing on the spot. Better understood, it is creating from prior knowledge and present awareness combined. This comparable attention to present awareness enables jazz musicians to connect better with listeners. Why? The listeners, along with the music and moment, are vital participants in the creation. Thus, jazz may assist ministerial leaders and all leaders to help persuade and empower others by building an attitude or perception that views congregants not as objects or targets but as co-creators, whose thoughts and ideas are to be taken as seriously as those found in any book or presented in any lecture.

Jazz Is Leaping into the Unknown and Learning to Love It

Cyrus Chestnut is one of the great jazz pianists of our time. Once before a performance, he began by apologizing to all of us in the audience. Chestnut said something that went like this:

> If you have come to hear us play some of our songs that have become favorites of yours, I am sorry, you probably won't hear them. And if you do hear them, I promise you they will not sound exactly like you are used to hearing them. We believe that each musical presentation is different and should be. We expect a song to sound different each time we play it.

So taken with his bold assertion, I spoke with Chestnut about it after the performance. He explained to me that though he prepared and rehearsed regularly and rigorously, he felt as though each time he performed, he was leaping into the unknown and, moreover, that he was learning to love it. A year or so later, I took a leap and asked Chestnut to play/preach my pastoral installation service at First Baptist Church, Tewksbury, Massachusetts. Not only did he come and play with great freedom and joy, but he spoke to us about not only daring to get out of our boxes but also daring to risk standing on them and jumping, and while in midair saying, "Wheeeee!"

Such wild appreciation for the unfamiliar and the unknown, such an effusive passion to push the boundaries of who we are and what we do, has the power to revolutionize a leadership ethos too often gone and grown stale. Mind you, what I am referring to is not just a recurring fancy for the hottest leadership fad. I am talking about cultivating a newness disposition not rooted in keeping up with fads but grounded in an understanding that God is Creative Newness, and that such an attribute is in our sacred DNA. Creative newness is not something we have to fear on the one hand, or fabricate on the other hand. Creative newness is something we simply must own and celebrate with more deliberate and sustained intention—in the spirit and way of jazz musicians.

To do so would be to unleash an era of pastoral leadership not just able to survive in a crazy-busy world as manic as it is meaningless for many, but to thrive in such a world, offering compelling energy, guidance, and vision sufficient enough to inspire and keep on inspiring new life.

For example, as leaders we may encourage each organization to attempt one new challenge each year and to do one thing they do annually in a new way. At the end of the year, all progress may be documented and celebrated in an "Annual New Creation Report." Though I am not one for encouraging the formation of yet more committees, there is something to be said for each local church having a Church Refreshing Committee. Their sole task would be to report on how the church is purposefully cultivating and sustaining freshness in ministry. Creative flourishing should not be left to chance in the church; it should be our utmost priority.

Jazz Helps Us Jump for Joy

Samuel Dewitt Proctor, beloved educator, pastor, and storyteller (at the height of his ministry, he is reported to have delivered more baccalaureate and commencement addresses than anyone), officiated at the funeral of jazz great Count Basie. He remembers the mourners being overcome with grief to the point of the service being in stark contrast and contradiction to the hard-swinging style "The Count" was known for. Proctor felt like he had to do something to change the spirit in the church. He called on the assistance of someone he himself had played with in a little jazz band at Virginia State College. That someone was none other than renowned and beloved jazz pianist Billy Taylor:

> I finally got the nerve to point to Billy Taylor, who was sitting in the front row. . . . The church was packed with musicians. "Please learn a little song for our dear and beloved Count Basie," I said. "It has only three verses, one line each, and you repeat it four times." Our organist, Dr. Jewel Thompson, played the tune through once and I spoke the words.
>
> *Woke up this morning,*
> *With my mind stayed on Jesus.*
> *Halleluh, Halleluh, Hallelu-u-jah!*
>
> Well, this great audience of jazz artists took hold of this little tune. (Samuel Dewitt Proctor, *The Substance of Things Hoped For* [Valley Forge, PA: Judson Press, 1999], 160)

Joy is a mighty source of energy for life and labor, including leadership. Anything is more doable with joy. And such doing yields the best work of all: being delightfully fulfilled in labor prior to responses and results. Joy nurtures not only work fulfillment but also work continuation and commitment. If we truly enjoy something, chances are, we will stay with it, discovering new adventures, leading to even deeper work joy. Fulfillment and commitment are contagious. This is a third potent blessing of joy for leadership. Persons are more likely to follow you if they are inspired. Deep joy and commitment fuel and fan the flame of inspiration.

If you truly want to be the best leader that you can be, loose the joy in you. Know and own those things that make you feel deeply happy to be alive. Do not feel ashamed of joy running over deep down in your soul. Remember, in addition to being alive, a blessing we didn't earn, don't deserve, and never saw coming, and in addition to the joy of fulfilling labor, we are living on the back side of resurrection of Jesus. Joy is the air of the new order. Amid all the wounding and heartache, there is a Relentless Healing Love at work in the world that will not be stopped, no matter what. Again, we are living on the back side of Jesus' resurrection! We do well to remember this more than one Sunday of the year. Speaking of the Resurrection, I once had this impression concerning jazz that I have not the will or the heart to recant: *jazz is the exclamation point to the Resurrection!*

Being Unusually Comfortable with Unusual Power

Perhaps because of our reverence of him as God's Son or our being used to his miracle-working ways, we have taken something amazingly significant about Jesus for granted: *his acceptance of living in divine strength as a way of life.*

Just think of some of the amazing things Jesus did that we tell and retell in Sunday school, Bible class, and sermons. We speak of such things as his turning water to wine, his walking on water, and his serving a gathering of five thousand with more than bread and water so matter-of-factly. And yet, such accounts do get remembered and retold. What is missing completely from the radar of our awareness and articulation is Jesus' being comfortable with the thought of playing with wonder; his risking embarrassment, not to mention extinguishment, by actually trying to do "the impossible"; and his continuing to live sanctified and sane in the wake of his works of might on behalf of mercy. Rather than be thrown off by his expansive energy and imagination, or routed into the dead end of ego-tripping, Jesus threw himself into wonderworking and making. He was unusually comfortable with his unusual power.

To live in divine power, we must learn to lean into divine power: to expect, sense, and trust our sacred strength. Amazingly, playfulness, the terrain of limitless make-believe and possibility, is wonderful conditioning for creating a lighthearted, all-things-are-possible mind-set, welcoming of everyday miracles. Given the mammoth challenges we face in our world, souls set free to face and fashion new creation boldly hold the greater promise.

When Jesus departed, he is reported to have said to his followers, "You will do even greater things." What if Jesus really meant what he said?

To be playful is to be powerful—increasingly so and beyond measure. Can you live with that? What I mean is that we are conditioned to be repetitive in ministry. In many instances, this year's church calendar is indistinguishable from that of years prior. The best we hope for is attracting new members with well-rehearsed programs. How might we imagine daring new programs that stretch us but also excite us in new ways? Such holy risking, in terms of new ideas, strategies, methodologies, and goals for ministry, offers the prospect for new ministry anticipation, excitement, and power.

What new (not for novelty's sake but for life ever new in the Spirit's sake) things are going on at your church?

How are you evaluating the effectiveness of the new programs?

How do you ensure that organizations and organizational leaders are being challenged by new thoughts and ideas?

How do you celebrate fresh, fun, and faithful ministry enhancements and initiatives?

Going from Dry, Dry, Dry to Alive, Alive, Alive

As I read the Old and New Testament I am struck by the awareness therein of our lives being connected with cosmic powers, angels and archangels, heavenly principalities and powers, and the groaning of creation. It's too radical, too uncontrolled for many of us, so we build churches which are the safest possible places in which to escape God. We pin him down, far more painfully than he was nailed to the cross, so that he is rational and comprehensible and like us, and even more unreal. And that won't do. That will not get me through death and danger and pain, nor life and freedom and joy.
—*Madeleine L'Engle,* Glimpses of Grace

Our daughter, Joya, sat next to me with a church bulletin in hand. She handed it to me and said, "Dad, it was all just dry, dry, dry." I read the bulletin given to her at the church she had visited that morning. I felt like I could have told her what was on it before reading it, and I could have. It read like most church bulletins I'd seen and helped to resubmit over and over

123

again. The "Order of Worship" was indeed ordered in such a way that all knew exactly what was going to happen, and what was to going to happen was exactly the same as what had happened too many Sundays before. Dry, dry, dry! Dead, dead, dead!

The challenge is deeper than refreshing worship. The challenge is to refresh our understanding about God, Jesus, and church, to catch exciting new visions of them. This means engaging in the holy play of daring to see God, Jesus, and mission in lighter and livelier ways. I catch hold of such faithful and fanciful re-visioning at play in the following passage from John Eldredge's magnificent book *Beautiful Outlaw: Experiencing the Playful, Disruptive, Extravagant Personality of Jesus*:

> To live in such a way that he is always something of an element of surprise, and yet, however he acts turns out to be exactly what was needed in the moment. Oh, his brilliance shines through, but never blinding, never overbearing. He is not glistening white marble. He is the playfulness of creation, scandal and utter goodness, the generosity of the ocean and the ferocity of a thunderstorm; he is cunning as a snake and gentle as a whisper; the gladness of sunshine and the humility of a thirty-mile walk by foot on a dirt road. Reclining at a meal, laughing with friends, and then going to the cross.
>
> That is what we mean when we say Jesus is beautiful.
> (John Eldridge, *Beautiful Outlaw* [New York, FaithWords, 2011], 137)

A spirit of playfulness set free in a church creates a more compelling and attractive environment, one that is more likely to awaken current members and, just as important, draw new members. Let's face it, the religious life is a major turn-off to a great many for a variety of reasons, including negative worship experiences, a sense that religious types tend to be too stuffy and overly restrained, and a belief that the religious are more interested in maintaining a tradition than they are in keeping up with the times. Sadly, all too often churches and church people have supplied and continue to supply sufficient data to support all of the foregoing claims. It is possible to be so focused on order and tradition in the church that we fail to appreciate God's great appetite for divine lunacy and surprise.

Playfulness has the power to unleash our innate spiritual capacities and longings for activities that are fun and that promote continued experimentation and growth. Freedom and forging forward are seen and experienced as natural and desirable.

The new congregational delight of which I speak is not driven by a hollow need to be considered a contemporary "cool" church. It is, rather, the enlivening overflow of genuine communion with a God of relentless creative spark and zeal. It is the result of individuals, congregations, and systems being filled and refilled by a Life Force that tends toward adventure, toward Advent. Advent ought to be more than a season in the church; Advent ought to be our way of life. So filled and fulfilled, the church becomes a place running over less with predictability and more with surprise, not because it strives to be, but because it is inspired to be. Such churches are places of unusual appeal for various kinds of people, who often can't articulate what it is that they are searching for, but they know it when they find it. These churches are sacred playgrounds with a compelling spirit that whispers and even shouts: *Come play with us as we play with God!*

Ministry beyond Your Vision: Trusting God with the Imaginations of Others

One leader could never hold the vision of God. God's vision is too grand for singular personal manifestation. Thus, the best of leaders know that their greater luminosity is in the shine of others. They are the leaders who have and feed a genuine passion for seeing others light up. The challenge is to make such a passion a priority of leadership. In order to do this, leaders must be willing to subjugate all, including all images of perceived success, to inspiring others to live their greater potential. The best support we can give people is to help them to become their best selves. This involves learning to trust and delight in trusting God with the imaginations of others.

There is no small tension in placing the flourishing of others above our visions of ministerial and organizational accomplishment and success. Yet, this is precisely what Jesus did by placing—risking and trusting—his vision for ministry first in the hands of twelve, and then tens more, and then thousands and millions more when he accepted his early death. He was able to trust that what was burning inside of him was bigger than he was, and that ultimately its full flourishing hinged on his ultimately trusting the One who had birthed the vision in him in the first place, to birth it and rebirth it in others. Jesus had to choose to believe that what would happen might not come out exactly as he saw it, but in the end, God's magnificent will, which always transcends all human comprehension and understanding, would be done.

Ministry is granted a fuller flourishing as we unshackle it from the bonds of our limited needs, desires, and dreams. While such realities ought not to be totally ignored, for they are as well sacred sources of divine insight and inspiration, our needs, desires, and dreams are not ever synonymous with the totality of God's vision. They always fall short of the elegant and ever-unfolding dream of God. With all due respect to impressive degrees and even more impressive titles granted and brandished among clergy, God's vision is best engaged as it is celebrated and distributed throughout God's dynamically diverse children, and not as it is concentrated in the voices of the "called" or the hands of the "chosen."

Great leaders freely trust God to inspire great vision in others and to manifest that vision in ways that are sometimes beyond the leader's wildest dreams. Such leaders, rather than being consumed by "the illusion of sole divine dream ownership," are lifted and even tickled by God's moving in mysterious ways beyond themselves. Take, for instance, the full wonder of the Resurrection: not only was Jesus raised from the dead, but so were his followers. They were and are raised from deadening limitation and fear to unprecedented heights of marvelous meaningful mission in the world. The Resurrected Spirit set fiercely and fancifully free that day— and each day since—is not just the Holy Spirit of one, but the Holy Spirit of many.

Perhaps the best inspiration a leader can give is to help persons become more aware of their inner flame and show by their living example that like the leader, they, too, can trust the fire that burns within. Brilliant leaders inspire others to discover their own brilliance. As truly inspiring leaders, leaders who see and fan the flame in others, we are called to allow God room to move in ways way past our being and our knowing. Rather than leading to a laxity and negligence about ministry, such widening of attitude and perception to include a vision of the fine and full flourishing of God's vision among God's people can create a dynamic new anticipation and excitement for ministry, transforming drudgery into thrill.

Ministry: Inspiring Others to Play Their Song Their Way

The following words by Wynton Marsalis hold a wealth of knowledge for pastoral leaders and all leaders:

> The most important thing you can do is to empower an-
> other person to be themselves—even if what they're going
> to do is going to be the opposite of what you do . . . you
> don't want to teach them dogma . . . you're a part of their
> story. A lot of times you [as a teacher] look at them as if
> they're a part of *your story*. You [should] try to empower
> them with tools to do what *they* want to do. (Nat Hentoff,
> "Playing Changes on Jazz Interviews," *Jazz Times*, April,
> 2007, 98, italics added)

So often, pastoral ministry is presented in just the opposite light. I can remember beginning my own ministry with
the intent to preach, teach, and lead people toward a model
of Christian witness that I had come to own as authentic and
true. Holding a vision of exemplary faith witness is an important attribute for leadership. Yet Marsalis raises the possibility of overholding such a vision. Overholding the vision, no
matter how applaudable the vision may be, makes us prone
to missing the vision God inspires within others for mission
and witness. Moreover, unconsciously subjugating the vision
of others leads to ministry with a heavy hand, the goal being to
implant our vision of faithfulness on others.

A viable alternative to ministry as imparting and impress-
ing our way onto the way of others is to understand ministry
first and foremost as inspiring others to play strong and true
the unique song God has given them to play. Such a perspective immediately lightens the load of ministry. Suddenly, we
are not obligated to change anyone or to persuade anyone.

Our job is not to carry around an ideal understanding of God's kingdom or kindom (thank you, Ada María Isasi-Díaz), begging and pleading with others to carry their share of the load. Ministry is seen as something much lighter and more manageable, if not downright enjoyable. The goal is to point and inspire, not push and pull. The job is to help persons to see and sing their own songs, in their own words and notes. And while there may be some general themes that we hope will be present (God's faithfulness, love, joy, and peace), we are relieved from the duty of forcing people to express faithfulness according to the exact mandates of some dogma or creed. Substituted for the weighty demand of prodding people to conformity is the far more delightful duty of observing persons express their own unique faith witness in compelling and surprising ways.

Seven Ways to Preach with a Lighter Heart

It had been a grueling week, and I had been up early that Sunday morning trying to piece together something that could at least be mistaken for a sermon, if not pass for one. I have long since forgotten what I said to the people that Sunday when I preached, but I have never forgotten what my wife said to me at home before I preached: "Enjoy your sermon." Her words stopped me. I wanted to say to her, "Yeah, right." I ended up saying, "Thanks, honey." As it turned out, I would have something for which to be deeply grateful. For the next weeks and months, those three words, "enjoy your sermon," remained with me, gently challenging me with the possibility of doing what I could do—and not leaving it to mood and chance—in order to make preaching a more enjoyable experience. Consider the following preaching joy-making strategies:

1. *See God in a more joyful light.* You may remember a popular song of the past entitled "He Ain't Heavy, He's My Brother." Spirituality does not need to be as heavy as it is often made out to be. Often, deep spirituality is seen as being synonymous with extreme weightiness of mind and heart: the true mark of a true believer is a deep-seated seriousness about God and life. But what if Divine Loving Mystery, or God, can be perceived with as much hilarity as heaviness? Given the wildly wonderful antics of God as presented in the biblical record—imagining a lavishly endowed world from absolutely nothing, turning a sea into a highway, sneaking up on life as an infant, giving death a taste of its own medicine—mirroring the holy heaviness while missing holy hilarity is a bad joke. In what ways do you envision and experience God's joyful nature?

2. *Embrace the joy of living.* I remember once cleaning my home office on a whim. I had not planned it, but before I knew it, I was moving this and placing that. Part of the unscheduled rearranging had me placing books I wanted to read over the next few weeks in a certain space, making sure my *Jazz Times* magazines were in order, and taking some things to the garage so that I would have more space in my office to do small things like breathe, stretch, and walk more freely. At the end of my cleaning and clearing, I remember standing in the middle of the room and saying to myself or hearing it said to me, "Enjoy." This impromptu benediction made me smile. What if the first and highest calling of all is to enjoy life? Presently, what are your five greatest joys?

3. *Treat yourself to lavish time for sermon preparation.* The great undoing of ministry in general, and preaching in particular, is busyness. Busyness is a bully in a number of ways. Not only will busyness repeatedly snatch valuable time for preparing a sermon away from you, but it also will drain you so much so often that when you do have the time, you lack the mental

energy to engage preparation freshly. Moreover, as sermon misses due to underpreparation mount, busyness will tease and taunt you into feeling shame and guilt about preaching below your own expectations, not to mention the expectations of others. The bullying of busyness ends up finally insulting you by making you feel bitter about the Sunday-to-Sunday obligation to preach, changing your calling from delight to drudgery. Develop or revise a sermon preparation schedule. Share it with a friend who will gently help you remain faithful to your schedule.

4. *Find the funny places in scripture; give the power of humor its due.* Legendary entertainer Bill Cosby once offered the following simple advice to the costars of his hugely popular television series: "Find the funny in it." I don't think that he was referring just to delivering lines that were meant to be offered up with a sense of humor, but also to an attitude and disposition that could easily and readily celebrate the lighter sides of any situation. Such advice is good for preachers to hear, especially when it comes to telling the same stories over and over again to some of the same people. Ideally, suggestions one through three will have the impact of seeing the funny in scripture without straining too much. Often, the funny will not be in the words but in the spaces between the words. For example, it is possible to perceive the funny by walking with God in the Garden of Eden, and imagining God and yourself being thrilled to no end by the surprising displays of vibrancy and vitality by creation and creatures. Or hear God calling Samuel at midnight in ways that would not make a child afraid but would make a child wonder and want to know, with more gleeful curiosity than grim suspicion, where the Voice was coming from. What makes you laugh easily and heartily?

5. *Be open to the contributions of the preaching moment.* The sermon is not something to finish and give to people; the

sermon is completed in the moment of preaching with peo-ple. I have discovered that there is more thrill to be had in preaching when I am not limited to what I have prepared to say and am open and alert to how persons and the preaching moment inform preaching in surprising and meaningful ways. Not knowing exactly how a sermon is going to come out need not fill you with angst, but rather anticipation. Mind you, such preaching lightness is not necessarily due to your carrying less into the pulpit (though such may be true to a certain extent), but more to your carrying what you're carrying more lightly. The point is less of a fixation on what you are fixed to say and more easy and gentle attention on what wants to be said in a moment of genuine sacred connection and communication.

Can you remember a moment when, while preaching, you added something to the sermon or subtracted something from the sermon? What was the impact?

6. *Resist preaching to answer and change.* I have linked my own increased joyfulness with preaching to an overhaul of my thinking about the purpose of preaching. I used to believe that better preaching provided persons with answers and the best preaching changed them. How awfully powerful! How impos-sibly burdensome! My present understanding regarding the goal of exemplary preaching is to see the preacher's calling es-sentially as Inspiring Imagination, Curiosity, and Desire about God, Gospel, and Life. The effect of this understanding on me is to practice preaching from a more spacious, gracious, and enchanting place. Once, I dared to preach about Judas—in the first person. Though the sermon dealt with a heavy subject— The Bitter and the Better in Each of Us—the impetus for the sermon was feeling graced enough to receive and be honest with the reality of my own bitter and better, and to do the same with Judas. Based on responses to the message, persons gave themselves permission to behold themselves, others, and

Judas in a more merciful light during and after the sermon. Preaching that sermon remains one of my greatest preaching thrills, for the excitement of it and, even more, for the faithfulness of it.

With this broader and lighter preaching intent, I can relax more knowing that my job is not to close the deal between God and God's people, but to be a part of the conversation, with no small joy. How do you debrief with God after a sermon? What is your experience of closure with a sermon?

7. *Be grateful for soulfully fulfilling labor.* I remember reading the phrase "work that is below our spirit." To be engaged in labor that drains more than it inspires is a tragedy. While preaching has and always will have its pressing demands, it can be immensely fulfilling and, dare I say, even fun. Personally, I thank God for the desire to love words, stories, and people. I am grateful for craftsmanship: the invitation to explore a labor for an extended period to points and places of discovering subtle but substantive nuance. It is joy on joy to engage labor that can be soulfully and repeatedly fulfilling prior to responses and results. Remember your calling to preach often. Regularly pour water on your preaching vocational choice. Find new ways to hug your calling, and your calling will find new ways to hug you back.

Holy Lunacy

Early one morning,

in the stillness

of being

held and loved

by God,

in my peripheral vision,

I saw

an angel

doing a cartwheel.

—KBJ

What the Swan Said One Morning

Take time

each day

to feed your soul

with something

other than obligation.

—KBJ

Morning Greeting

This morning,

while praying,

I passed by

several angels playing,

each one

greeting me,

in the same way,

"Good Morning,

Child of God."

—KBJ

A Play Prayer for Theological School Graduates

I pray for and with these graduating,

yet still journeying

students of wonder and word.

May they be gifted with ministries that are

faithful and uncanny, and

holy and whimsical.

And, should their spirituality become

too isolated, lofty or stuffy,

let them remember

the lighthearted dance of the Nazarene,

whose liberating work

erupted at a wedding feast

and ended at a seaside fish fry.

Finally, for now, Marvelous Holy One,

Who loves us all madly,

Please continuously mess with their

"Master of Divinity" degrees

so that sometimes they will read

not "Master of Divinity," but rather

"Magic of Divinity"

Or

"Melody of Divinity"

Or

"Mystery of Divinity"

Amen.

{ LIVING FULFILLED ON STILLNESS, AWARENESS, AND PLAYFULNESS }

When fear comes,
start laughing with God.
—KBJ

Stillness: Widening the Space for Awareness and Playfulness

One of my biggest reasons for writing this book was to examine and explore how three undeniably potent life-giving resources in my life informed and affected each other. My suspicion was that such mighty powers, having One Great Common Origin, would have identifiable and interesting convergences. My hope was and is that cultivating a better understanding of how stillness, awareness, and playfulness inform each other directly and indirectly will inspire deeper appreciation and desire for both their unique expressions and their points of magnificent convergence. The first point of convergence I wish to identify is the blessing of stillness for awareness and playfulness. In a word, the blessing is spaciousness.

We have lived in the same home for almost twenty-five years. I remember the very first time we visited the split-level ranch house in Randolph, Massachusetts. My wife and I were immediately impressed with the large number of rooms. The owners were parents of several children, and the house somehow felt livable for parents, siblings, and friends of siblings. Next, my wife, a wonderful cook and baker, fell in love with the solid oak cabinets that almost made a half circle around the kitchen. As she continued her enchanted beholding, I began to do some of my own on the back porch just off the kitchen. Several large windows conspired to offer a view of a backyard that was three times as big as any we'd seen at other homes we'd visited. As I looked out onto the vast expanse, I imagined our children running and jumping freely and fancifully in this mini-neighborhood playground. In mid-imagining, my wife joined me on the porch. She easily and fondly recalls what I said to her when my mind returned from its play in the yard: "This is it."

What I understand now to be so compelling to me on that back porch almost two and a half decades ago is the same reality I believe makes increased attention to and practice of stilling so important. In temporarily clearing out as many words and thoughts as possible, stillness makes room for free human understanding, expression, and engagement. Such spaciousness makes for a wider range of perception and understanding. Subsequently enriched understanding seeds desire and, just as important, confidence, to undertake new adventures that stretch and transform us.

Stillness breeds spiritual, mental, and emotional openness, essential new room to imagine fresh thoughts and explore novel possibilities. The greater the stillness, the greater the possibility for thinking thoughts we haven't thought before, and risking embarking on daring explorations—the best play of all—we never imagined before.

Understanding the richer value of spaciousness for human flourishing and transcendence, is it any wonder that where there is astonishing sacred manifestation in the Bible, there is usually lavish holy spaciousness? In the beginning God, who is Freedom, plays unhinged and unhindered in a vast field of nothingness, and new worlds emerge. Moses is invited to see what God sees in an open plain on the back side of a desert, and a relentless spirit of liberation is unleashed in the land. Amos thunders, "But let justice roll down like water, / And righteousness like a mighty stream" (Amos 5:24, NKJV) in the Spirit of a God who would see prosperity widely disbursed among all his creation. There is no keeping down God's tendency toward expansiveness.

Consider Jesus. Though respectful of religious tradition, according to the witness of the Gospels, He will have little to nothing to do with those domestications and restrictions associated with it that diminish the human holy spirit. Once he senses it is time to, before something unspeakable breaks inside of him, Jesus makes a break for the wilderness, where he finds his cousin and fellow space walker, John, waiting in anxious wonder for him. This same Jesus keeps breaking out, whether it be while openly addressing boisterous winds and waves on a storm-tossed sea, or while wistfully using the ordinary around people (like mustard seeds and lampstands) to explode the extraordinary inside of people, or while stretching so wide and broad in the sleep of death that he feels more alive than ever before and takes to the open road again, free and easy like Sunday morning. Jesus keeps breaking free.

Do you sense the connection between his broad power and the lavish spaciousness of his soul cultivated by regular periods of time spent in stillness and solitude? Was Jesus endowed with much, because he was committed to making provision for much? What if the essential prerequisite for such awesome endowment is emptiness? Is there any limit to what God can do through a person with an open, willing, and trusting heart, a heart more regularly conditioned and moistened by stillness and the openness it brings?

Openness may very well be the single most important and least talked about value of leadership. We speak so much of needing to have this skill and that understanding, yet as significant as any learning is the ability to relinquish all that we know, that we may be able to engage as best we can each fresh moment with a fresh mind. Of course, this does not require that we forget all we know, but that we harness it so that it in no way diminishes or dulls our experience with new insight. Thus, momentary unlearning is crucial for continued maximal learning and growth. As much as we can be enhanced by what we know, we can be held back by what we know.

Miles Davis once instructed a guitarist to play a certain selection "like you don't know how to play the guitar" (Kidder and Todd, *Good Prose: The Art of Nonfiction* [New York: Ramdom House, 2013, 9]). The guitarist admitted to being initially confused but then amazed, as he played the song beautifully in a way he had never played it before. Davis's profound advice speaks to the need to keep what we know at bay intentionally so that prior knowing has no negative impact on our capacity to know in wonderfully new ways. One might call this going back between knowing and not-knowing a kind of sacred play.

Awareness: Bringing Light and Love to Stillness and Play

I believe that stillness and play are richly experienced for the sheer vitality of them on their own terms, with no goal in mind whatsoever. They are holy ends in and of themselves. But part of their overall value is that both may be enhanced by deeper reflection. This is the point at which we may understand how it is that awareness makes a valuable contribution to stillness and playfulness.

Awareness supplies insights for pondering in moments of stillness. We have delicious opportunities not just to hear more clearly ideas, unimpeded by competing sounds and pressures of life, but to catch them in midair and connect them and create new ideas. Awareness not only fills stillness with prospects for creative wisdom connecting and formulations, but it allows for a more vigorous integration of life as action and life as reflection. Henri Nouwen addresses the value of personal reflection for a more fulfilling life:

> A life that is not reflected upon isn't worth living. It belongs to the essence of being human that we contemplate our life, think about it, discuss it, evaluate it, and form opinions about it. Half of living is reflecting on what is being lived. Is it worth it? Is it good? Is it bad? Is it old? Is it new? What is it all about? The greatest joy as well as the greatest pain of living come not only from what we live but even more from how we think and feel about what we are living. (Henri J. M. Nouwen, *Can You Drink the Cup?* [Notre Dame, IN: Ava Maria Press, 1996], 26)

Awareness brings to play a critical dimension that helps us to play in ways that inspire rather than diminish life. Perhaps one of the reasons play has not been given its proper priority in the apprehension and practice of spirituality is precisely because of so many ways that we are able to play poorly. Negative experiences have led to a whole series of phrases presenting unpleasant reality in playful terms:

143

Stop playing.
Don't play like that.
He's just a player.
Don't play me for a fool.

Play is too potent a reality to let popular formulations that decry its reality take the day. Awareness is what keeps us imagining and creating play that's not just about satisfying selfish agendas, but co-creating, with others, the beloved community. Through awareness, we are able to envision and play in love, for love, with Love.

Playfulness: Resisting Taking Stillness and Awareness Too Seriously

What surprises there are! We are such planners! We decide how God must come into human affairs. We treat it all with a kind of public relations twist. We pick the time and the place. We insure that the right people are there to meet God. We get the news releases out as to what to expect. We even have some prepared quotes. But God has an uncanny way of taking care of times and places and entrances. While we wait at the airport, as it were, with a representative committee of dignitaries, an escort waiting for the coming, God has a way of quietly arriving at the bus station, walking up the side street, and slipping, unnoticed, through the servant's chambers.
—Gene Bartlett

There is a dynamic loving Holy Spirit delightfully free in the universe, ever seeking to encourage, heal, and surprise. Gene Bartlett's assessment illustrates for me the ways we are prone to tame spirituality with expectation, familiarity, and preference. His crisp indictment highlights the way we can suck the surprise out of God, with beliefs about God that conform ultra-strictly to our familiar and comfortable notions of God. Winking and grinning, playfulness shouts that God is always beyond our highest notions and fondest preferences.

Playfulness keeps our stillness and awareness honest and fresh. Playfulness challenges any offering of stillness and awareness that does not keep God fanciful, and free, beyond our wildest dreams, and ever new.

Playfulness also keeps us humble, saving us from thinking we can ever save ourselves by ourselves, no matter how holy we think we are or can ever be. Speaking of being, Alan Jones's observation in *Sacrifice and Delight: Spirituality for Ministry* is a keeper:

> God's delight is that we should simply be. . . . What drives us is the desire to be. What drives us mad is the desire to be everything. God's delight is to share the divine life with us, so much that we human beings are called to be the Shepherd of Being. ([San Francisco: HarperSanFrancisco, 1992], 143)

Not only does playfulness season the aspirations of stillness and awareness with humorous humility, but it saves the heavy tone and somber style of too much overdone religiosity. The spiritual life as it is often billed and illustrated can be so off-putting. Realities that are paraded as being invaluable for life can be presented in such lifeless ways.

A playful spirit ensures that our times of stillness and awareness are as lighthearted as they are enlightening, and that when we seek to share what we have learned, we are as likely to sing and sway in dancing ease as we are to say anything at all. Playfulness keeps stillness and awareness in play for the faithful fun of it.

Fulfillment: Living God's Dream

Regularly practicing stillness, awareness, and playfulness cultivates a disposition of fulfillment. In part, this means that the flavor of all three may be experienced separately or together at any time while doing anything or not doing anything at all. A common experience of this is momentarily feeling as light as a feather and like you are on top of the world, for no apparent reason. Some fear owning such moments, erroneously linking them, I believe, to impending doom. In damning dark ways, too many have been conditioned to live not expecting to enjoy. Living suspicious of joy may begin in childhood, as a life of constant turmoil leads one to believe that life is supposed to be more sorrow than happiness. The first portion of Paul Laurence Dunbar's immortal poem "Life," from *The Complete Poems of Paul Laurence Dunbar*, comes to mind:

> *A crust of bread and a corner to sleep in,*
> *A minute to smile and an hour to weep in,*
> (New York: Dodd, Mead, 1980)

Yet joy keeps coming. Such moments are characterized by stillness—time seems to stop, awareness—we are suddenly overcome with an extreme and overwhelmingly satisfying sense of the lightness of just being, and playfulness—we feel as though we could fly.

Such moments need not be the exception, and such a thought regarding their sustainability need not be a pipe dream. What if living continually replenished is God's dream for us? It is certainly a vision in keeping with the way of a God who loves lavishly and unconditionally.

Given the proper resources, starting with stillness, awareness, and playfulness, is this living so fulfilled something worth considering as persons, as leaders? How might daring to live fulfilled continually empower us to inspire others toward faithful and creative ministry in a crazy-busy world? Imagining dynamic continual empowerment is the first step toward receiving and trusting dynamic continual empowerment.

Such empowerment finds a cheerful witness in the second part of Dunbar's poem, which concludes on verbal notes of "joy" and "laughter."

And that is life!

Choosing Fulfillment

Some of my greatest moments have been thirty thousand feet above the ground. I'm not referring to piloting or skydiving, but to coming upon a soaring insight while reading aboard a plane. One such moment occurred some years ago when I read the following words in *Man's Search for Meaning* by Viktor E. Frankl:

> We who lived in concentration camps can remember the men who walked through the huts comforting others, giving away their last piece of bread. They may have been few in number, but they offer sufficient proof that everything can be taken from a man but one thing: the last of the human freedoms—to choose one's attitude in any given set of circumstances, to choose one's way. ([New York: Washington Square Press, 1959], 86)

The effect of this passage on me was akin to a person recognizing for the first time that she possesses a treasure of immense worth. Though an adult for many years who had made countless choices by the time these words befell me, up to then I had never beheld the enormousness of being able to choose, to decide, to create my fate. I had not considered the sacred magic of choice to create anything—anything at all—even in the most dire of conditions. Indeed, Frankl reveals to us a wonder of wonders: prisoners turned sacred mages of their own destiny.

Frankl's witness invites us to consider our power to choose as being at the heart of our divine sacred strength. To behold and learn to utilize such holy power fearlessly is to honor our inner sacred mage. As God's children, we are all sacred mages invested and trusted with a divine wand of choice. The effect of this on us is agency given to us: the means of exerting vital energy and influence, no matter what we face, including the ability to join God in transforming any situation into a reality of barely speakable healing grace.

As a Christian, I see Frankl's glorious example of inner strength as being in keeping with what is perhaps Jesus' greatest unsung contribution to religious and theological imagination: daring to envision continual and unusual vibrancy as abiding within the sacred home of one's own soul. What else do you think Jesus had in mind when he said, "The kingdom of God is within you" (Luke 17:21, NKJV)?

Choosing to own our dynamic inner strength of being able to choose transports us to new levels of creativity and resilience in everyday life. Through imagining and wielding such inner strength, we can resist bowing and breaking before any challenging predicament. We can know and live that the choice is always ours either to accept circumstances that we're given passively, to curse circumstances bitterly and give up, or to choose actively to create new circumstances and give it our all.

Don't Be Afraid of Oh, My God! Flourishing

"April in Paris" is a beautiful ballad. Yet it can be made to swing and swing well. If you don't believe me, give a listen

STILLNESS, AWARENESS, AND PLAYFULNESS

to the song on the album *Ella and Oscar*. Ella Fitzgerald and Oscar Peterson were unsurpassable at their respective gifts. On this song, and indeed the entire album, there is evident the attitudinal disposition that made their formidable talents soar: they were not afraid of flourishing. Listen to "April in Paris," and you hear their not being afraid to explore freely and celebrate the full ranges of their imaginations and musicianship. The result is a sacred explosion of creativity and merriment. The improvisational soloing that begins about three minutes in is Oh, my God good!

There is Oh, My God! flourishing in each of us. We were not born merely to find our purpose; we were born to playfully fashion and happily flourish in our purpose.

Peter Gomes, gone too soon, was an extraordinary preacher who served as minister of Memorial Church at Harvard University for more than three and a half decades. I once heard him joyfully confess his frequent response to inquiries concerning his well-being: "I flourish!" Gomes didn't just answer with the usual "Fine, how are you?" His "I flourish!" I am sure caught many unfamiliar with it and the ultra-lively Gomes off guard.

Why shouldn't we own and lean into our flourishing? What if human flourishing is God's dream for us?

You Don't Have to Feel Full to Be Full

The eleven disciples went away into Galilee, to the mountain which Jesus had appointed for them. When they saw Him, they worshiped Him; but some doubted. And Jesus came and spoke to them, saying, "All authority has been given to Me in heaven and on earth. Go therefore and make disciples of all the nations, baptizing them in the name of the Father and of the Son and of the Holy Spirit, teaching them to observe all things that I have commanded you; and lo, I am with you always, even to the end of the age."
Matthew 28:16-20 (NKJV)

149

In the final chapter of the Gospel According to Matthew, Jesus promises to be with His disciples forever. He tells them this after having returned from the dead. According to the text, the risen Jesus is, in fact, speaking to a mixed crowd of believers and doubters. Why wouldn't there be doubters? A man came back from the dead, just like that! Perhaps the doubters feared, and not unjustifiably so, that the gathering on the mountain that evening was a setup to do away with as many followers of the dead Nazarene as could be done away with at one time.

Just a little less amazing to me now than the surprising arrival of the Resurrected One is the fact that Jesus does not divide the crowd before making the promise. You and I may have been tempted to separate the crowd into "believers" on one side and "doubters" on the other side. Perhaps we would have made the promise of continual spiritual companionship to the believers alone. But amazingly and graciously, Jesus does not split the group into two smaller groups, and the great big present of a promise is offered to all present. Jesus doesn't need the doubters to be with him, for him to be with them. Similarly, God's being with us does not hinge on our being with God. Oh, how wonderful that is, because it's exactly when we don't feel close to God that we need God's presence the most.

My very first car was a Dodge Coronet. I remember picking it up one Saturday morning. As I trekked home, however, I had one of the most frightening experiences of my life. While I headed home on a four-lane highway, it began raining fast and furious, not just "cats and dogs," but "lions, tigers, and bears." As I nervously searched for the seemingly hidden switch to turn on the windshield wipers, I began to pray. My prayer was quick and to the point. When you're in trouble, you don't pray long prayers. I prayed, "Lord, please don't let me wreck my new used car!" I kept on praying, driving, and looking in the rearview mirror. The reason why I kept looking in the rearview mirror was because my father, who had taken me to pick up my new used car, was right behind me all the way, trailing me home. Knowing that my father was with me, no matter what, made all the difference in the world.

The power of God's Presence makes all the difference in the world. It may even be the reality that makes this book make the most sacred sense to you. Perhaps during its reading you've wondered if anything, including stillness, awareness, and especially playfulness, can create a continual flourishing and thriving attitude in ministry. Aren't the contemporary demands of leadership much too complex and crazy busy to allow us to think we can do anything other than keep our heads above water?

Given the biblical witness offered at the beginning of this book, especially those images of flourishing linked to water, such as the words of Jesus promising that out of us will flow "rivers of living water," a life and leadership model of thriving ought to be kept alive as promise, if not practice.

Yet we have something more than promise and potential practice going for us. God is already flourishing and fabulously alive in God's being. If we truly believe as we teach through our understanding of Pentecost that God is as much God within us as God is God outside of us, the implication is enormous: the flourishing power and potential of which I have been speaking, primed and potent for living and leading, are already within you. We have God's Presence within us going for us, the extent to which perhaps we have never given ourselves permission to imagine before.

It is ours to claim and cultivate unusual wisdom, peace, and joy, which are already strangely but surely planted in us, through God's abiding Presence.

No Need

There is

love limitless

and

grace boundless

and

therefore absolutely

no need

at all

to worry.

—KBJ

For Once and for Always

The one

and only

one thing

God wants

from any

one of us

is to let

ourselves

be loved

for once

and

for always.

—KBJ

Hallelujah Declaration

There is a continual lavish flow of grace within each of us that, when freely experienced through stillness, awareness, and playfulness, endows us with a boundless abundance of wisdom, peace, and joy.

Slap Wild Wonder

High five the sun

as it shines

and the rain

as it falls,

and the breeze,

as it blows.

Slap the wild wonder of God

playing full and free

in fanciful ways!

—KBJ

About the Author

Born in New Orleans, Louisiana, as the second son to the late Frederick and Ora Mae Jones, Kirk Byron Jones is a graduate of Loyola University and Andover Newton Theological School. He holds a Doctor of Ministry degree from Emory University and a Doctor of Philosophy degree from Drew University. Dr. Jones serves as adjunct professor of ethics, preaching, and pastoral ministry at Andover Newton Theological School. Throughout his thirty-year pastoral ministry, Dr. Jones has served on various religious and civic committees at the local and national level.

Jones is an increasingly sought-after speaker, preacher, and teacher in a variety of venues across the United States. His writings have been published in various journals, including *The Christian Century, Leadership Journal, Gospel Today, Pulpit Digest,* and *The African American Pulpit,* a quarterly preaching journal he cofounded in 1997. Jones is known and beloved for his continuing ministry with seminarians and the clergy, and is often called "The Preacher's Teacher."

Before answering the call to serve in academia, Dr. Jones served as a preacher, in a variety of local church settings. He was the founding minister of Beacon Light Baptist Church in New Orleans. He served as Senior Minister at Calvary Baptist Church, Chester, PA; Ebenezer Baptist Church, Boston, MA; and the First Baptist Churches of Randolph, Whitman, and Tewksbury, MA.

Jones is the author of several best-selling books for those seeking to grow spiritually in an ever-challenging world. His jazz/poetry-influenced work strikes a chord (or touches a nerve) with readers of all ages and places in life. "His writing resonates with me," says fellow author and pastor Adam Hamilton, "and it reminds me of things my soul craves, but that I too often forget in the midst of my daily life."

Dialogue with Dr. Kirk Byron Jones on Facebook at:
"Yes to Grace" and "The Sacred Seven Group"
and on Twitter at "Kirk Byron Jones"

Also by Kirk Byron Jones

Rest in the Storm: Self-Care Strategies for Clergy and Other Caregivers

Addicted to Hurry: Spiritual Strategies for Slowing Down

The Jazz of Preaching: How to Preach with Great Freedom and Joy

Morning B.R.E.W.: A Divine Power Drink for Your Soul

The Morning B.R.E.W. Journal

Holy Play: The Joyful Adventure of Unleashing Your Divine Purpose

Say Yes to Grace: How to Burn Bright Without Burning Out

Say Yes to Grace: The Facebook Page Reflections

The Sacred Seven: How to Create, Manage, and Sustain a Fulfilling Life

DISCOVER AND DEVELOP THE FULL
POTENTIAL OF A PERSONAL
AND ORGANIZATIONAL

{ FULFILLED MINDSET }

FOR
YOURSELF
YOUR LEADERSHIP TEAM
YOUR CHURCH
YOUR ORGANIZATION

FOR INFORMATION ON FULFILLED COACHING,
LEADERSHIP TRAINING, CHURCH AND ORGANIZATIONAL WORKSHOPS,
AND CONFERENCE PRESENTATIONS,
VISIT WWW.KIRKBJONES.COM.